THE 7 PILLARS OF A NOBLE WOMAN

Becoming a Woman of Distinction

SYLVIA S. BANKS

This book belongs
to
A Noble Woman

The 7 Pillars of a Noble Woman Becoming a Woman of Distinction

ISBN 978-1-941749-50-0
Library of Congress Catalog Number 2016910913

Cover Design: MS Design & Photography
Photographer: Matthew Henry
Interior design: Laura Brown

4-P Publishing
Chattanooga, TN 37411
Printed in the United States of America

Dedication

This book is dedicated to two beautiful women. You may never read about them in history, but they are a part of my story and who I am today.

To my loving mom, *Pramila Devi Suganandam,* you are an amazing woman. I honor you for your faith, strength, and virtue. You have worn many hats and excelled in everything you set out to do. Most importantly you were a role model for me, and I appreciate what you taught me by your lifestyle. I am eternally grateful for my godly heritage and foundation. I love you and thank you!

To my wonderful mom-in-love, *Martha Logan Banks,* thank you for receiving me and loving me as a daughter. I appreciate you for raising a man who loves and serves God with all his heart. He values family and treats me like a queen! What more could I ask? I am so blessed. And how can I forget, I learned how to cook Southern soul food from you. I love you and thank you.

Table of Contents

Foreword

Sylvia Banks is a remarkable woman. She carries the anointing and wears the spiritual clothes of a truly noble woman. She has much to share with women who desire to move away from the perversity of this culture to the holy dignity of God's design for them. Her story and instructions are inspirational!

~Dina Rhoden, MSN, Ph.D, Compassion House

This book is a gift Sylvia is presenting to women. I am proud of the way she worked through her insecurities and fears, pushing through to the end. This book is a must read. Every woman has the hidden treasure of being a noble woman. As women read this book, they will discover what is inside of them so that it can be manifested on the outside.

I honor Sylvia for taking the time to discover the noble woman inside of her. It has been a blessing to me as her loving and supportive husband, and to our children. Her influence has placed an indelible mark on our lives. Sylvia, I am grateful for who you are and all you do to serve your family and community. I will always love you!

Your noble king,
David

Acknowledgments

To David - God knew exactly who and what I needed when He brought you into my life. Thank you for loving and supporting me in all my endeavors. Thank you for encouraging me to write this book. You are my best friend, and I enjoy sharing my life with you. I look forward to all that God has in store for us.

To my precious children- Ben, Caleb, and Maiya: What a privilege and honor to be your mother. I love each of you dearly. You bring such joy to me, and I am so proud of each of you. Thank you for being my technical support team!

To my parents- Harris and Pramila Suganandam: I am at a loss for words, I don't even know how to begin to thank you for instilling godly principles and truths in me. You have been such incredible role models for me throughout my life. I am so blessed!

To my siblings - Praveen and Betsy, Nalini and Mark: You guys are amazing! I could not ask for a better brother and sister-in-law and sister and brother-in-law. I will always treasure the precious time we spend together. Thank you for your prayers and encouragement. (My precious twin niece and nephew: Ian and Malaika, I love you!)

To Dina Rhoden - Thank you for taking time out of your busy schedule, and volunteering to edit. I appreciate your encouragement and kind words. Thank you for placing the commas in the right places.

To my volunteer team - Nalini and Georgie: Thank you for your time and willingness to proofread and polish my manuscript. I appreciate your insight and suggestions.

To my "War Room" partners - my praying sisters at Catoosa Homeschool Co-op: I value each of you, and appreciated your prayers during this process of writing.

To my Empowerment Church Family - I love each of you from the bottom of my heart!

To Laura Brown -Thank you for being obedient and creating S.W.A.T. Book Camp. You are such a gifted teacher. You inspire me, and I appreciate you! Thank you for helping me to reignite my passion for writing.

Above all, I thank God for creating me to be who I am. I am unique; I have value, and I am noble. I cannot take credit for anything in my life. I am humbled to be God's instrument and a voice to women who may be in the desert of their lives. God is the author of my life!

Preface

As I began this journey to write a book, I had no idea that it would include an autobiography.

My focus was on you the reader and not me, the writer. I wanted to pour out to you what was in my heart. Sharing tidbits of my life experiences to help you. I love helping people, and I desire to see people and especially women live up to their potential. You will discover that there are several practical tips and tools for you to use and implement in your life.

Then one day, I started writing my story, and before I knew it, I had typed twenty-five pages. I set it aside, thinking I would just pull stories from it to sprinkle throughout the book. Somehow, I couldn't seem to fit it all in. I shared the manuscript with my editor and a few others. The response was the same from each of them. They all encouraged me to include it as part of the book.

As you read through it, I hope you will find it encouraging, funny and interesting. I want you to see how God orchestrated my life. He has always been and continues to be the beacon of light in my life. I also want you to see the gift of a godly heritage and foundation that shaped my life. I understand not everyone has that foundation. And perhaps you can identify with that. You didn't grow up in a godly home with Christian values. There is nothing we can do about the past, but I want to give you hope that you can start a godly heritage right now, with where you are. Build a solid foundation for your children, grandchildren, and the generations to come. They will rise up and call you blessed.

Dear friend, your story will be different than mine. But, I want you to know that God is a part of your story, too. Every twist and turn is a part of your destiny. It's a part of who you are and who you will become.

For years, I had this book buried inside of me. I dodged and avoided opportunities to dig up this book and put it into writing. My excuse was the time factor, but little did I know that behind that lame excuse was the real reason, the fear factor. I had allowed the fear of rejection to stop me from writing.

You see, I used to write. I would write little devotionals and place them on the table for our clients to pick up and read. They were words of inspiration and hope. Many clients appreciated these weekly devotionals and found them to be helpful. One morning, as I walked into the office, I noticed that all the devotionals had disappeared. I was a bit surprised. I remembered seeing a stack of them just the day before.

I shrugged my shoulders and went about my daily routine. I picked up the mail and went to deliver it to the gentleman who also shared our office. He was not in his office, so I placed the mail on his desk. As I turned around to walk out, my eye caught something yellow in his trashcan. I recognized the pieces of paper and realized they were the devotionals that I was missing earlier. They had been discarded in the trashcan. I was angry and hurt! This man was a leader, a spiritual man, and someone whom I looked up to.

That day was the last day I wrote. I decided I was never going to write again, and if I did, it would never be good enough. I allowed that image to replay in my mind time and time again. Nothing was ever mentioned about the devotionals, and after a time, I just forgave and put it behind me.

Maybe someone has crushed your dream. Perhaps you have been discredited in some way. I don't know what you may have experienced. The enemy will use the senseless, and painful things that people will do to deter, and delay us from fulfilling our purpose. Once you realize his strategy, it's up to you to fight against it and move forward.

I made up my mind, as we began the New Year, I was not going to allow fear to stop me anymore. I signed up for the S.W.A.T. writing class. I had the support and encouragement from my family, and friends. They were not going to let me give up. It has been nine months of dedication, and commitment, roughly the length of time of true pregnancy. And after birthing three wonderful children, I know the joy that comes from pain and labor.

This book is a buried treasure that has emerged and has finally been birthed. I had to see beyond my insecurities and self-doubt. I had to remind myself of my purpose and the vision God had given me. I realized it wasn't about me, but rather being obedient to God and allowing Him to pen this book, through me. And He has done it, and I give Him all the glory.

What about you? Do you have a "treasure" you have buried? Someone is looking for that treasure. They need it, and you have been hiding it. Don't wait any longer. What you have been given is for such a time as this.

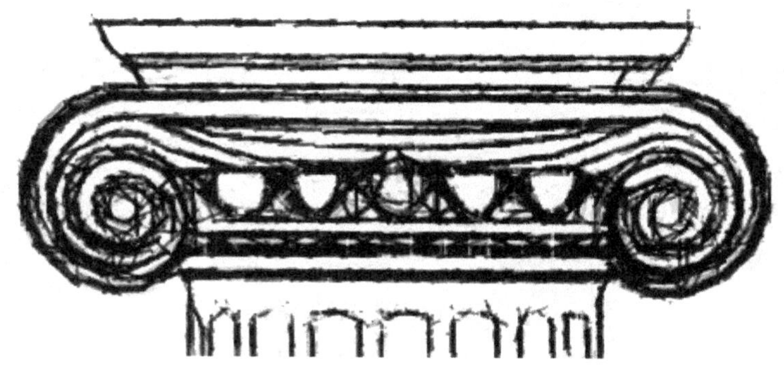

My Story - The Making of a Noble Woman

My upbringing was different than most people. I was born in Addis Ababa, Ethiopia. For those of you who might need a little geography lesson, the country of Ethiopia is located in East Africa. My parents, who are of East Indian descent, were serving the Lord as missionaries, so that made me an "MK," a missionary kid. We were a unique family because it was more common for missionaries to go to India, than for Indians to become missionaries. My parents were trailblazers, and their lives reflected the God they served with passion and fervor.

I was so blessed to not only have a godly heritage and upbringing but also to be surrounded by people of faith. We lived on the college campus where my dad was a professor. The other families that lived there were from different countries. My childhood friends were from the States, Sweden, Germany, Norway, and the local Ethiopian kids. We became one big family on that college campus. What brought us together was the call of God, and what kept us together was the love of God.

The Search

At the age of six, my parents sent me to a boarding school. Education was important to my parents, both being educators themselves. However, the options in the town we lived in, Debra-Zeit, were slim. All the local schools were taught in Amharic, the local language, and my parents felt I needed to be educated in English. Well, I can remember this particular day like it happened yesterday. We drove into the big city, the capital city, Addis Ababa, and went from school to school. There were several options, but which one was going to be the best choice for me? We stopped at the Norwegian, Swedish, German, and French schools. They were all boarding schools, and they were willing to enroll me in their schools, but I would have to be educated in a new language.

The day was long and exasperating, even for me as a six-year-old. I had no idea what it must have been like for my parents. They wanted the best for me, and yet what was that best? My dad was totally against me going to India for my education. That's what many of our Indian friends had done, and in some cases, the separation was devastating to the families. My relatives would have welcomed me and cared for me, no doubt. But dad felt it was too far, and our family needed to be closer in proximity.

Looking back, it is clear that God had His hand on our family and directed our steps. Someone mentioned a school to my parents where missionary kids attended. It was outside the city limits of Addis Ababa. They suggested that we give this school a try. It was a boarding school, and the teachers spoke and taught in English. The name of the school was Bingham Academy, which still exists today.

My parents made the necessary connections, and before too long we were at the school, taking a tour and talking with teachers. Everything seemed to fall into place. Bingham was the school that fit and met our needs. My parents were thrilled and of course, praising God for providing this school for us.

It was summer, and we spent our summers in India every three years for three months. That whole summer we prepared for my transition to first grade at Bingham Academy. We were given an extensive list of clothes, linens, and items to bring to school. Everything had to be labeled and have name tags on it. My parents could not find a place that would print cloth name tags so that they could be sewn onto my clothes. My genius parents ordered a rubber stamp with my long name on it: *Sylvia Suganandam.* They purchased some India ink, a stamp pad, and some cotton fabric. Dad neatly stamped my name in rows on the fabric. Then the fabric was laid out on the terrace to dry, anchored with stones. It did not take long to dry in the hot, Indian heat. My mom cut the labels out, folded the raw edges and sewed them. *Voilà!* DIY, (do it yourself) name tags. My new clothes, linens everything I owned now bore my name. There would be no question when the laundry was being sorted whose clothes belonged to whom. As a six-year-old, I was so proud of all my new stuff and the label with my name. These were my things, and they belonged to me.

Boarding School

Our hot summer in India came to an end. I have never dared to ask my parents how much they spent on me that summer. We arrived in Ethiopia, and it was time to pack my little suitcase and head to my new school. We headed to the school; it was probably an hour drive from our home. There we were the four of us, Dad, Mom, me and my younger brother. All the other families were arriving, too, everyone carrying suitcases, barrels, and trunks.

As I was recollecting this event in my life, it hit me that I did not know a single soul in that school. I had met the headmaster; he was a tall, bald gentleman and I had met my first-grade teacher, Miss McDonald, but other than that I did not know one student. There was no one anywhere near that school that even looked like me. I was the only Indian kid. That was not an issue to me at the time because I had grown up with so many nationalities around me.

Well, my parents helped me get settled in by unpacking my stuff. I was sharing a room with eight other girls who were also first or second graders. My dorm mom, Miss Frieda Riddle, had carefully labeled everything for us. We knew exactly whose bed was whose, whose drawers belonged to whom. Our names were clearly marked where our towels and toothbrushes were to be kept. Everything had a place, and everything was in order. To this day I follow the same pattern.

One would most likely describe me as a quiet, shy, timid child. I liked to follow the rules and stay out of trouble. I did not like to make mistakes and would rather learn from the mistakes of others. So, this was an adventure for me and very much outside my comfort zone.

Miss Riddle announced that it was time for the parents to say their goodbyes and leave. As my courageous parents hugged and kissed me, something in me went off like a lightbulb. In my six-year-old mind, I had not connected that dad and mom were leaving me. Suddenly, I was overcome by emotions, and I realized that this was not a good idea. The picture in my mind is vivid as I type this, and my eyes are clouded with tears. I screamed, "Mommy!" and as I ran after them, my loving dorm mom grabbed me in her arms. My parents too were shocked; I was not a child that had outbursts like this. They turned around puzzled not knowing what to do. Miss Riddle assured them that I would be fine, and it would be best for them to leave. A thousand thoughts flooded through my mind. Suddenly, I did not want to be left behind! I wanted my parents!

The Rhythm of Life

Needless to say, I calmed down and probably slept very soundly. I don't recall what the next day was like. My life fell into a pattern, a rhythm of sorts. We were awakened at a certain time. We got dressed, and the mornings could be a little chilly in Ethiopia. Our classroom was at the bottom of the hill, so we ran as fast as our little legs could carry us to our classroom. There, Miss MacDonald was waiting for us with a little heater. We plopped ourselves around her on the cold wooden floor. She taught us Bible verses that we committed to memory. We learned passages at a time. When our Scripture memory time was over, it was time to run back up the hill and make our way to the cafeteria. We ate breakfast and then headed back to our dorm rooms where we had to make sure our beds were made, chores were done, and that we brushed our teeth. Once we finished our tasks, we headed back down the hill to begin our school day. The routine and getting acquainted with my roommates helped me with my homesickness.

It was years later that my parents confessed to me that the night they left me, they sat in their car at the school gate crying and wondering if they should leave me. Reluctantly, they drove to a friend's house to spend the night. I guess that way, they were only minutes away from me, just in case they needed to come and take me home. This took place in the early 1970s in Africa, so technology was far from being advanced. We did not even have a telephone in our home nor did we own a television. We had a radio, tape player, and record player. Because the friends they stayed with that night lived in the capital city, they had the luxury of having a landline telephone. They called Miss Riddle and asked her how I was doing; they told me later. She informed them that I was fine and happily playing with my new friends. When my parents shared this with me, years later, I thought no, I was not fine, my little body was trembling from crying so hard, and I needed you to come and get me. But God had a plan, and I spent the next three years of my life attending Bingham Academy. My brother joined me the following year.

We were so fortunate to be able to go home on the weekends. The political situation at that time in Ethiopia was not good. The regime of Emperor Haile Selassie (The last emperor of Ethiopia, who reigned from 1930-1974.) was coming to an end, and the reign of communism and red terror was taking over the country. Everything was being rationed, and supermarkets and stores only had empty shelves. Gas was rationed, and everyone only received so much gas in their cars. The idea behind this was to keep people from traveling on the weekends and especially from going to church. They were given enough to last them to get to work and back. Since my parents lived on campus, they were able to save their gas and they made a commitment to come and pick us up each weekend or every other weekend.

I looked forward to Fridays. I would have my little black bag packed and head to the front of the school, the main building, and wait on the porch for my dad to arrive. I am not sure how we managed without cell phones. Our only means of communication was through letter writing. I would see my dad pull up, and I would rush out to meet him, jump in the car and off we went. I probably talked his ear off, telling him my weekly news and all that had happened at school.

The Question
"What do You Want to Be?"

It was during one of these Friday evenings on our drive home that my dad asked me a question. It's a natural question that parents ask their children, but the answer I gave him astounded him. He pulled off to the side of the road and turned around to face me in the back seat. He couldn't believe his ears, so I guess he thought he had to look at me to see if I was really serious. My dad tells this story over and over again in his teachings and sermon illustrations. He says, "I asked, my daughter: Sylvia, what do you want to be when you grow up like mommy?" He says, "I thought she would say, a doctor, nurse, or teacher, but you know what she said? She said she wanted to become a missionary. I slowed the car down and stopped on the side of the road and turned around to ask her my next question. Do you know what a missionary is? She said, Yes, daddy, a missionary is someone who tells others about Jesus. I asked her, who told you this? She replied again without any hesitation, "My teacher."

I do remember that night and that conversation, and I was as serious as I could be. Our teacher had been telling us about people who lived in remote areas of the world who had never heard about Jesus and how missionaries had gone to these people to reach them with the gospel of Jesus. Something stirred in me even as a six-year-old, and I knew that is what I wanted to do. I wanted people to know Jesus and live for Jesus. I remember my friends and me befriending an Ethiopian girl outside the school fence. She would watch us play on this dangerous tire swing that was so popular. I was not the adventurous type, so I stayed a safe distance from it and spectated as my friends risked their lives. They would pull the swing up to a hill and then hang onto it with their hands, push off the hill and swing way out into the woods, several feet off the ground, and then jump. Nope, that was not for me; I stayed where it was safe. Anyhow, the local kids would watch us through the wired fence, and usually, we would just ignore them. There was one particular girl that we befriended, and since I was the only one who could speak fluently in Amharic, I was the spokesperson and translator. We decided to ask her if she knew about Jesus and we proceeded to witness to her. She had some black twine around her neck, like a necklace, which we were convinced was witchcraft. So, we told her she needed to ask Jesus into her heart. I remember we prayed with her and wiggled our little hands through the fence and broke the twine from her neck. We might have seen her a couple of times after that and then she never came back. We were serious about sharing Jesus. We never told anyone that story, for fear we would get in trouble for going too close to the fence and talking to a total stranger. But, I do wonder at times, whatever happened to that girl and if what we said even made sense to her. I hope that I see her in heaven, and we can both have a good laugh.

An Encounter with the King

I told you my upbringing was different. The political situation in Ethiopia began to deteriorate. We witnessed the emperor being driven to his prison cell and did not know that it was him in the little VW bug. My family had met the emperor in Debra-Zeit. We were driving to the local store to buy popcorn for a fun day at the college. We could see that ahead of us cars were being summoned to stop, and people were getting out of the cars and lining up along the road. So, my dad pulled to the side, and we all got out, and as we were doing so, the police informed us that the emperor was on his way to his weekend retreat by the lake. We knew he had a palace there and had heard that as he gets close to the palace, he would get out of his car, and walk the distance with his motorcade following close behind. Along the way, he would greet whoever was standing and bless the children by laying his hand on them and give them a crisp brand new dollar bill. Well, that happened to us. He greeted my parents in the Indian fashion by putting his hands together and then shook their hands. He laid his hands on my brother and me and gave us each a crisp dollar bill, which my parents still have in their possession. Wow! What an experience! We were not even dressed to meet the king; we were just in our casual attire, and there we were in the presence of a king!

...and there we were in the presence of a king!

My parents did not stop talking about this for days--umm, let's say weeks! Dad said he was never going to wash his hands and everyone that he told the story to, wanted to shake his hand, the one that touched the king.

The New Government

Okay, so back to my story, but, I just had to tell you about the meeting with the king. If we had Facebook or Twitter then, you know it would be all over social media. Unfortunately, the college where dad taught was taken over by the new government and was going to be converted to a military base. Our perfect little world was changing fast. Our friends were leaving the country, headed back to their homelands. There were many teary-eyed goodbye parties. One by one everyone left, and we were still there.

Once again, the hand of God was on our lives. By this time our family had grown and I had a baby sister. She is eight years younger than me, so I felt like I could take care of her. My parents did not think it was an option for us to go back to India. They felt they had dedicated their lives to help the people of Ethiopia, and that's what they were going to do.

An opportunity opened for my dad to take a teaching position at the seminary. The seminary was located in Addis Ababa, the capital city. So, we packed up our stuff and moved into our new home and lived on the seminary campus. There were families from various countries, and we became fast friends with everyone. There was a good Christian school just minutes away from our campus, so my brother and I attended there as day students. That year our faith was tested, and we experienced some crazy things as a family because of the political unrest. It was as if the enemy was after us to destroy us. Our home was broken into one night, and we literally could have all been killed, but we were spared. My dad and baby sister were captured by the government and thought to be some kind of spies because of a plot by people rebelling against the government. They were found not guilty and released. My mom was teaching at a local government high school and nearly got shot because at any given time anywhere someone would fire a round of shots. We heard gunfire throughout the night and heard trucks carrying dead bodies. We heard horrific stories being told. We saw bloodshed and things you did not normally see. As kids, we were afraid, and we begged our parents to leave the country. Even our Ethiopian friends encouraged my parents to leave. They would say, "This is our country, we have nowhere to go, but you can go to your country." Still, dad and mom refused to leave; they were determined to weather this political storm with their Ethiopian brothers and sisters.

Communism took over, and we saw a flood of Russians and Cubans come into the country. The school we were attending felt it too dangerous to stay open, so they closed their doors that year. We went back to Bingham Academy. I was now in the fifth grade. Bingham was no longer a boarding school because most of the missionaries that were stationed in remote villages had fled the country. Bingham opened its doors and welcomed many of the diplomat's children. These were the ambassador's children who were in Ethiopia representing their country. We had our own United Nations right there on that campus. We had kids from Asia, Europe, the

States, and several African countries. These kids did not come from Christian homes, but they learned the Bible and heard about Jesus from our loving and caring, teachers every day.

Bingham was a great school for me and gave me a biblical foundation. As an observer, I watched my instructors and staff. They conducted themselves in a godly manner and were so kind, loving and giving. Our family was able to build relationships with them and we fellowshipped together over meals. Even years later, we kept in touch through Christmas cards and letters. Many of my elementary teachers are now in heaven. I will be eternally grateful for the seeds they planted in my life.

From Bingham to Rift Valley

I graduated from Bingham Academy completing eighth grade. Bingham did not have a high school, so the question came up, what now? The political situation had somewhat stabilized. Again the options were slim. We heard of a boarding school in Kenya, another country in East Africa, and several other families had sent their children there for higher education. Rift Valley Academy (RVA) was like Bingham, but on a much larger scale. The majority of the kids that attended there were missionary kids, and they came from all over Africa. The teachers and staff were from the States, England or Canada and they were dedicated to teaching missionary kids.

Now, to get from Ethiopia to Kenya, one must

fly. The flight was only an hour and a half. After, five years of living at home, it was time to go back to being a boarder. This time, the distance would be greater, and there would be no weekend visits. The school calendar was set up in such a way that we had three months of school and returned home for about a month. We flew home for Christmas, Easter and then a little longer visit for summer. The transition was much easier. I was older, and I also had a lot of friends who would also be going with me. It so happened that we went to India for our summer vacation just before I started at RVA. Almost like *déjà vu,* there we were again, shopping off the school list to get me ready. Everything was neatly labeled, and when the day came, I flew to Kenya. The director of the seminary in Ethiopia, where my dad was teaching, was traveling in India that summer. So my parents coordinated our flight schedules, so I would not have to fly such a long distance by myself. They were staying on in India for a few more weeks and would head to Ethiopia directly.

It was about midnight when we arrived in Nairobi, Kenya. I was exhausted! A gentleman from RVA was there to meet me. I don't remember too much about our ride to the school. It was about an hour drive from the airport, and it was bumpy. Finally, he took me to my dorm room. Everyone was fast asleep. My friend from Taiwan, whom I had gone to school with at Bingham, was one of my roommates. She had kindly made up a bed for me.

I'm not sure who informed my parents that I had safely arrived. We lived by faith. I am so grateful for the advancement in technology.

Classes had already started, so I had a bit of catching up to do. The campus was huge, and there were a lot of students. My life fell into a pattern. There were guidelines to follow and rules to abide. To me, that had been my way of life, so I welcomed it. Tell me what I am supposed to do and where I am supposed to be and I am there. I am a rule follower.

We had a young couple who were our dorm parents. They were a lot of fun and kept their apartment door open to us. I believe this is the time in my life where I matured. My sheltered world was not so sheltered anymore. I became more aware of the world around me. I realized that just because people said they were "Christians," it did not mean that they always acted like Christians.

> The decisions and choices you make not only affect you, but they also affect others, especially your family.

My heart began to hurt for my peers and the students around me who were making choices and decisions that were not good. I couldn't understand why they just continued to disobey the rules. It seemed simple to me if you are supposed to be in your dorm by 9:00 p.m., why in the world would you want to stay out later or worse yet, sneak out? Just follow the rules.

I had been taught well by my parents that the

decisions and choices you make not only affect you, but they also affect others, especially your family. Dad often quoted from the book of Proverbs, "A good name is to be more desired than great wealth. . ." I was too afraid to do anything that would bring dishonor to God or my parents.

I corresponded with my parents regularly. I titled my letters as epistles because that's where I poured out my heart to them. I don't think they even make them anymore, but they were called aerograms, an envelope and writing stationary all in one. You wrote on it and folded it up, licked the flaps, and *voilà*, you had an envelope to address, stamp and off it went. So, there were a lot of blue aerograms that went back and forth from Kenya to Ethiopia.

One of the highlights of my high school years at RVA was the "Spiritual Emphasis" weeks that we would have. Special guests would come and tell their testimonies and invite us to pray the prayer of salvation or rededication. It was during one of these weeks that I felt a stirring re-dedicate my life to God. I had asked Jesus to come into my heart when I was either five or six, and I had sincerely meant it. But, I realized that I had to make my faith my own. I could not rely on my parent's' prayers or their faith. It was time for me to develop my personal relationship with God. I went forward that night and stood with a crowd to say, "Yes, Jesus, I will serve you. I am yours. Tell me what you want me to do." We were given little blue cards to write the date on to tuck away in our Bibles as a reminder of that life changing night. I knew something changed in me, and I felt so good. I wrote my parents and shared my experience with them.

I was still a pretty quiet gal and did not get involved in too many things. I found a little job working at the school infirmary and also at the library. I learned to cut hair and would trim hair for my friends and brother. I served on the student council for a season.

The Next Step

Remember, how I told my dad I wanted to become a missionary when I grew up? Well, I was beginning to question God and seek His advice. I just knew I wanted to help people and especially women, and I didn't quite know how to follow up with that desire. Academics was ok, for me, I was not your brainiac. I was more artistic and creative and enjoyed classes that emphasized these aspects.

My parents would have loved for me to pursue something in the medical field. They did encourage me to consider nursing. I just knew I was not cut out for that kind of work. Hospitals, sickness, and blood just gave me the heebie-jeebies. So, I was not going into the medical field, plus you have to be able to do math and science. Those were not my strong subjects.

I really and truly had my heart set on returning to India and attending college there. I wanted to major in psychology and set up a counseling center and help women. After my junior year at RVA, my brother and I flew to India to meet up with my parents for our summer vacation. We looked into a few options for me to attend college. Indian school systems are set up according to the British system. They were not willing to accept my American education and said I would have to repeat a year or two of high school to fulfill the requirements. We did not think that was wise and decided that God had closed the door. But, we did not know where the next door would be.

Just because time was running out and all my friends were applying to colleges in the States, I decided to give it a try. Remember my parents were missionaries, so how in the world could they afford to send me to the States to attend school. It was a miracle that both my brother and I were able to attend RVA. There were times when the school bill had been past due, and my parents were prayerfully wondering how to pay the bill. I kid you not; it was in those times that God showed up. We received notes from the school office stating that our bill had been paid anonymously. We did not know whom to thank, but God. God sent financial blessings at different times in our life, so we knew, we just had to trust Him.

The Other Side of the World

I applied to a couple of colleges in the States. I

had friends who were attending Bryan College, in Dayton, Tennessee. They were girls I grew up with on the seminary campus, so I felt good about going somewhere where I would at least know someone. This was the work of God again in my life. The family who lived next door to us on the seminary campus were from the States. Two of their girls were a little older than me, but we became good friends. Their uncle was the academic dean at Bryan, so they decided to attend there and encouraged me to apply.

I heard back from two colleges which accepted me. One was in New York, and the other was Bryan College. Bryan offered me a scholarship that would cover my tuition. My parents were responsible for my room and board. So it seemed like the best choice. I couldn't imagine living through the winter in New York.

My senior year came all too quickly. My parents and siblings attended my graduation. It was bittersweet. For four years RVA had been my home. There were special friendships that were formed and as classmates we had become like family. Now we were all headed in different directions to make our mark in the world.

I spent that summer in Ethiopia with my family. Preparations were underway for my journey to the United States. I would be the first person from my immediate family to have ever set foot on American soil. I had my passport and needed to obtain an American visa. The United States had tightened its regulations, and it was harder to obtain a visa. So we were aware that this would determine God's will for me to pursue my higher education.

My dad and I drove to the American Embassy with all my documents. I was sure my dad would be with me through the process, but the guard informed us that only the one requesting the visa was allowed to enter. Dad gave me the documents and said he would be waiting for me. I was given a number and had to wait my turn. The building was full of people wanting the opportunity to experience the "American Dream." The officers were stern as they asked individuals questions as to why they wanted to go to the States. Some people received the stamp of approval and others the stamp of rejection. I was nervous as I watched this scenario. Finally, my number was called, and I handed the officer my documents. He looked over my papers, saw my acceptance letter from Bryan College, asked me a few questions and stamped my passport with a visa. Wow! I was going for real now. I thanked the officer and went out to look for my dad. He had parked his car along the side of the road. I got in the car and told him I got the visa. My dad was so happy; his response was, "Thank God." I knew he had been sitting in the hot sun that day praying for me.

The day came to say goodbye to my parents and siblings. This time, I was flying across the world. We did not know when we would see each other. My parents are remarkable; how could they have such strong faith and trust? This is the kind of foundation they gave me.

We took a very scenic route to the States. My two friends had come home from Bryan for summer vacation, so it worked out for all of us girls to travel together to the States. We had some friends in Europe, so we stopped in Norway for a few days. It was a long and tiresome journey. Did I tell you flying is not my thing? We were welcomed at the airport in Chattanooga, Tennessee by my friends' uncle and aunt. They were the sweetest people and even told me I could call them uncle and aunt, which I did. I thought *this is America!* It was a long drive to Dayton. I couldn't see what America looked like; it was already night and quite dark. We pulled up to the dormitory and a kind lady let us in and showed us our room.

Bryan was the perfect place for me. The campus was beautiful, and the hills and landscape reminded me of Ethiopia. Dayton was a small town, so I adjusted to my new atmosphere and what would be my home for the next four years. There were students from other nationalities, and several others were MKs (Missionary Kids) like me. I did not feel too different or that I stood out like a sore thumb. God had been preparing me for this time in my life.

God showed Himself in so many ways; it would take volumes to record each detail. He provided friends who became like family to me and took me home on breaks and vacations. He protected me and blessed me with good health as I adjusted to the seasons especially winter. He provided financially and met all my needs. I was able to work on campus at the library.

One of the highlights during my time at Bryan was after my freshman year; my mom was able to come to the States. She had been asked to become the librarian at the seminary and would you know it, that year there was a library conference being held at Bryan. Only God could have orchestrated that. She received an invitation to attend the conference. Her trip was paid for, and the best thing mom, and I got to spend time together. I will never forget her visit.

The following year, my brother came to the States and attended Bryan as well. The summer of my sophomore year, we both flew back to Ethiopia. We were like celebrities; everyone wanted to see us or meet us. It was everyone's dream to come to the States, so those who would probably never be able to come wanted to experience it through our eyes. It was wonderful to be home for those few months. You don't realize how much your family means to you until you are separated from them.

Again, I became keenly aware of the hurt and pain around me. When people found out I was majoring in psychology and that I was aspiring to become a counselor, they were interested in setting up a time to talk with me and share their life. I didn't know what God was doing in my life or what He was preparing me for. I just wanted to help people. I focused on my education and decided once I graduated; I would head to India and set up a counseling center. That just seemed like the practical and sensible thing to do and pursue.

Boy Meets Girl

God was orchestrating another plan that I was not prepared for. There was a nice guy on campus that seemed to be in all my psychology classes. He came in as a business major and then switched to psychology. We had a few conversations and spent time studying together occasionally. He was curious about my background and was fascinated about India. He had never met an Indian girl before.

There was something unique about this guy. He was sincere and serious about his faith. The more time we spent together, the more, we realized that we had similar passions and pursuits for our future. He wanted to help people, and you would often see him around campus talking or praying with other students.

Our friendship grew, and we felt that God had brought us together, and so we considered what the future would be like as we moved towards engagement and marriage. I shared this news with my parents, and you have to understand because of our Indian culture, they were a little shocked. You see, their marriage was arranged, and I believe that's what they were expecting to do for me. I wanted to be as transparent as I could with my friendship and relationship with David. They were across the ocean, so all they had to go by was what I told them about him.

David came from a great family. His parents were believers and were actively involved in their local church. He grew up in a small town outside of Atlanta, Georgia. He had two older siblings, which made him the youngest. I had opportunities to meet his family and as most parents would, I am sure they had their questions and doubts.

We both had a strong spiritual foundation, and we are so grateful for that. There were so many things that we found we had in common. There were also things that could divide us, our cultural differences for one. Although I am Indian, I did not grow up in India. I evolved with a culture of my own having lived in Africa and being raised in a multi-cultural atmosphere. So, that left me a little confused as to what was expected of me. Naturally, we wanted to be respectful and honor our parents in every way possible.

Life after College

And so, we did. I graduated from college, and my parents attended my graduation. This was my dad's first visit to the States. He had often dreamed of coming as a young man for further education and to pursue his dreams. But God had another plan; his children would come first, and he would later come to celebrate their accomplishments and dreams.

Dad and Mom had a chance to meet David, and they liked him a lot, but they still were not sure about the marriage thing. For one thing, we were still so young. David still had one more year left in college. They encouraged me to go on and pursue my master's degree and stay focused on my education. There was also the issue of my legal documents to remain in the country. I was only here on a student visa, and that gave me permission to be in the States for four years.

I spent the summer with my parents. We toured around Washington, D.C. and New York and saw all the amazing historical sites. We visited with friends and family. My parents headed back to Ethiopia, and I returned to Dayton to figure out my life.

I discovered that I could extend my student visa for one more year if I was able to get a job within my field. This was considered practical training. I applied for everything I could. I moved from Dayton to Chattanooga and rented a room from a friend. There were more job opportunities available in Chattanooga, so I spent days interviewing and job hunting. Finally, I landed a job.

My last straw of hope: I applied at a daycare. I will never forget that series of events. I talked to the director over the phone. She was extremely interested and asked me to come in for an interview. We set something up, and you should have seen her face when I walked in the door. She was not expecting an

Indian girl to show up. Mind you, having grown up in a multicultural setting, I did not have an Indian accent. By now, I had also probably picked up a southern drawl. So, this poor lady was assuming that I was a Caucasian American.

Well, needless to say, the interview went well, and I was hired on the spot. The paperwork was taken care of, and I was now legally allowed to work. My first real job. This job was a real eye opener for me. I was hired to teach the pre-kindergarten kids. There were about 20 of them. Most of the teachers there did not think I would last long. These kids were undisciplined, not all of them, but most of them. And at 5' 2" and barely 115 pounds, yep, they could have taken me down. But God was faithful. I was able to take control of that class.

This experience was eye-opening for me. I was working in a secular environment. I was totally shocked about their lifestyles of my coworkers and the way they talked. I saw the devastation and hurt that comes from divorce, separation, and unhealthy relationships. It was evident in the lives of the kids. They were starving for affection, approval, and significance. I was not prepared for all of this. I did my best to love these kids and bring structure and order in their lives. Because we were a secular daycare, we were not allowed to mention God or anything spiritual.

David was in Dayton finishing up his last year at Bryan. We kept in touch through phone calls and letters. We tried to see each other over the weekends. We still felt strongly about our relationship, but we were determined to have our parent's blessings before we could move forward. We committed ourselves to praying for God's will to be done. I remember telling David that if he chose to leave the relationship, I would totally understand. We could part as friends. I did not want him to feel that he was stuck, so I gave him a way of escape. He refused to take it and decided to wait patiently for the green light from my parents.

> This was a match made in heaven!

The Green Light

It was a brisk September morning, and I decided to call my parents. I talked to my mom for a little while. Dad was not at home, so she said they would call me later. They did, and we talked for little while just catching up on this and that. I did not mention David, just because it was a sensitive topic, and I did not want to upset them. Well, interestingly, they brought him up and asked how he was doing. And then, suddenly, out of nowhere, they said, "We have been praying, and we are giving you the green light to go ahead and plan your wedding." What?! Did I just hear what they said? I had to pinch myself to make sure I was not just dreaming. I tearfully told them thank-you. I knew this was a monumental step of faith for them and me, too. No one in our family had done something like this out of the cultural norm. And I was the oldest child on both sides of the family. So, in a way, I was setting the standard for others to follow.

Of course, as soon as I got off the phone, I called David. He answered and all I could do was to cry. He thought I was hurt, or something terrible had happened to me. I finally managed to get the words out and shared the good news with him. We both realized at that moment that God had answered our prayers. We knew that this marriage and our union was far bigger than us. God was setting the stage for us to discover our purpose and fulfill the destiny He had ordained for us. This was a match made in heaven.

Our wedding took place on June 30th, 1990. Our families and friends were there to celebrate this great occasion with us. We did our best to marry the Indian and American cultures together. Most importantly, we wanted to glorify God because it was He who had orchestrated all of this. We were just participating in a grand plan. My dad spoke so eloquently at our wedding, sharing that this was a marriage of families and cultures. It was such a beautiful day, and everyone that was there could feel the presence of God. David and I were so thankful that we chose to do it God's way. We followed the principles and to this day we reap the benefits of blessings from both sides of the family.

There we were a newly-wed couple. David got a job working at Teen Challenge as a counselor, and I continued with my work at the daycare. We worked opposite shifts, I worked early in the morning and was at home by early afternoon. He left just before I got home and worked until late in the night. We barely saw each other, so our communication was mostly through letters and cards we left each other.

Faith in the Wilderness

We were happy but knew God had much more for us in store. After all, we both had college degrees in psychology, and we were anxious to use all our knowledge on the world. We decided Chattanooga was too small, and we needed bigger and better opportunities. So, without a lot of thought or wise counsel, we packed up all our belongings and headed to Atlanta. We soon discovered that the world doesn't care about a bachelor's in psychology. You needed experience or better yet a master's degree. So, we found ourselves in the same boat. David found a job at the mall, and I was able to transfer to a daycare that was in the same network.

We call this our wilderness journey. Just like God took care of the children of Israel in the wilderness, He took care of us. We found a church that we liked and attended. The pastor had just started a series of faith, and he spoke on that topic for the six months we lived in Atlanta. We realized that Atlanta was too big for us, the dynamics of our family were about to change, so that caused us to rethink a few things.

The last Sunday we were in Atlanta, the pastor finished up his series on faith. We knew that was not coincidental, but rather God's plan to get us back on course.

Baby on Board

Teen challenge readily hired David back, and now that I was pregnant, it was too hard for me to find a job. I did find some part time employment working for a photography company, setting up appointments. We were welcomed back to the church we had left. The pastor asked us to head up the counseling center for the church. This was like a dream come true. Everything we dreamed about was coming true. David resigned from Teen Challenge and went to work for the church full time.

We had no idea how great the need for Christian counseling was. David worked hard and would often have 50 to 60 sessions a week. He counseled married couples, families, and many single ladies. I helped with office work and sat in on sessions with him when he counseled women. Our center (LifeLine Counseling Center) was located away from the church. This gave us a great opportunity to reach the community as well as people in the church. Again, the realization of pain, hurt, disappointment was manifested as we heard people's stories. I was blown away. I knew people had issues but did not realize the magnitude of pain that people suffered. Remember, my life had been so sheltered and protected.

Our baby boy was born, and we were thrilled to be parents. We very quickly discovered that kids don't come with a manual. I remember the first day we arrived home from the hospital, Benjamin, started to cry. I called the hospital and told the nurse the baby was crying, and I was not sure why. She kindly told me that he either needed to be changed or be fed. No one had prepared me for motherhood. For that matter, no one had prepared me for wifehood. I found myself struggling to balance these roles.

My mom was far away, and I had spent a majority of my life in boarding school, so though I had learned a lot from my mom, there was a lot I did not learn. I did not have women in my life at the time to mentor or guide me. I truly felt all alone. And still being a little shy and quiet, I did not know whom to talk to.

Marriage and Parenting

David and I also felt that we needed to make sure our marriage was strong. We both had unrealistic expectations. Our cultural differences surfaced at times. We realized we both had different perspectives on marriage not that one was wrong, or one was right. We were both viewing it from different angles. We were quick to remedy anything that could potentially tear us apart. We wanted a godly marriage and family. We didn't want to settle and be "just married." We wanted to enjoy every aspect of marriage and follow the design and pattern that God had laid out in His Word.

We took the time to invest in our marriage, and we attended marriage conferences. We learned and applied so many great tools. We also comprehended the blueprint for marriage and realized it was okay to be different. We could respect our differences and celebrate them. We also attended parenting conferences, because we wanted to be the best parents we could.

We gained so much knowledge and revelation. We were passionate about helping marriages, and I was drawn to helping women. We conducted marriage seminars and classes, and I developed two courses to help women embrace their identity and to bring order into their homes.

Leaving the Zone

We were in a comfort zone. Everything in our world seemed perfect. The counseling ministry was going well. David had also been asked to serve as assistant pastor. Our family had grown, and we had two sons and a daughter. Our boys were attending a Christian school. I was able to help David at the office and care for our infant daughter. David had not only been able to complete his master's degree but also his doctorate. We felt somewhat settled. Life became a routine, and our faith was not being challenged or stretched.

The soft feathers of our nest were slowly being removed. The boys' school closed its doors due to funding. A shifting was taking place at the church. After twelve years we were feeling uncomfortable. David especially was feeling very unsettled and restless. There were so many things he wanted to do at the church and for the church. He was not given the opportunity to implement his ideas.

We sought the Lord and wondered what was going on. During this time of restlessness, we lost David's father. He had been sick, but we did not expect him to pass away. The pressures were heavy on David's shoulders so that he did not even have time to grieve the loss of his dad. We thought perhaps these feelings of unsettledness would disappear, but they did not. They only became stronger.

A New Beginning

David did what he only knew to do and God gave him peace. He resigned from his position at the church as director of LifeLine Counseling and also as an associate pastor. David was the only counselor at LifeLine, so if he left that would be the end of the counseling center. Our pastors were not necessarily thrilled, but they were gracious to bless us and pray for us for whatever God would have for our future endeavors.

That was one of the toughest moments of our lives. We walked away from everything that had brought stability and comfort to us. We would no longer be receiving a paycheck, and we had just left our "family." These were the people we had grown up with over the last twelve years of our marriage. Although we questioned God, we also had a sense of peace.

David decided to launch his counseling and consulting practice. He set up an office, and he had a steady stream of clients. We visited other churches but just could not get rid of the unsettling feeling. Then, one day, David shared with me that in his prayer time with God, he felt God instructing him to plant a church. We were both baffled. That's the last thing we wanted to do. We had seen enough of what goes on behind the scenes of the pulpit, and we wanted nothing to do with that. Besides, there were over 800 churches in Chattanooga, literally a church on every corner. Why in the world, another church?

We fought the feeling for several weeks. We needed wise counsel. David called a friend, who was a godly man. He shared what was going on with him and asked the man for his counsel. The man was attentive and offered to pray with us about our situation. He promised to get back with David. Well, he did. He confirmed to David that God had indeed called him to plant a church. The reason we could not feel settled sitting in the pew was that a shepherd cannot become a sheep. This was such a revelation to us, and we were awestruck. But it made perfect sense.

My husband tells the story so much better than I do. But we had nothing to start a church with. No money, no people, and no building! How in the world were we supposed to start a church? We knew better than to argue and fight with God, so we said okay, we'll do it.

We shared with our boys, Ben, and Caleb, what we were going to be doing. They were so supportive of the decision we were about to make. Maiya was still a baby so; we couldn't talk to her. We held church in our home those first few Sundays. It was just the five of us. We worshiped to music on CDs, and David preached his heart out to the boys. Maiya tended to get a bit fussy just as the sermon was about to begin, so I usually had to step out of the room with her.

In time people started inquiring about what we were doing. A few families were interested in visiting our church. By this time, we had moved the church from our home to David's office. They had a small conference room that we could set up. Slowly we started growing. We outgrew the office and held services at a community recreation center. That was quite an experience. We would get there early Sunday morning. The place would be filthy from the activities of the weekend. We would clean and mop and set out the chairs. It started out with just David and I doing all the work. Eventually, others participated and helped us. It was a lot of work, but we were at peace knowing that we were in the will of God.

Our season at the recreation center came to an end, and we moved to an old church building downtown. The place had been sitting dead and empty for years. We went in and scrubbed and cleaned the place. We continued to grow. All was going well, and then the boiler at the church broke down. It was a cold winter, and there was no way we could heat the building up. The organization we were renting the building from did not want to invest the money in fixing the boiler.

God provided a ram in the bushes, and we moved to another location. This place was huge, and it was clean. We were ecstatic. We had classrooms, a place large enough for fellowship gatherings and a huge area for worship. The rent fit our budget. God continued to bring people to the church. We were so humbled and knew this had nothing to do with us and everything to do with God.

If you recall, I shared that the boys' school had closed. We did not know where to send the boys for their education. We did not want to send them to public school, and we certainly did not have the means to send them to another private school. The ministry was able to provide a small salary, and it was enough to cover our basic needs. David continued to do counseling and consulting on the side to help ends meet. By this time, we had decided that I would be a full-time, stay at home mom. We were willing to make the sacrifices; our family was much more important to us.

Banks Academy of Excellence

We decided to give homeschooling a try. We committed to one year hoping it would give us time to find the perfect school for our kids. We did not know a lot about homeschooling, but we decided one year would not damage our boys. We had friends who also had boys that were the same age as our boys. They too were affected by the Christian school closing; we set out on this homeschooling journey together. The blind leading the blind. The name of our "school:" The Banks Academy of Excellence.

As I write this, I can tell you that our year of experimentation with homeschooling has added up to almost 16 years. We have successfully graduated our two sons from high school. Ben graduated from college and Caleb is halfway finished with college. Maiya, our youngest will be entering the ninth grade. We are very proud of our kids. Looking back, we see that God planned the events that would take place in our lives for a reason. Homeschooling gave us the opportunity to invest into our children, not only academically, but spiritually as well.

My Season of Purpose

I felt like I had some experience now. During this season of becoming a wife and a mother, I read several books by notable Christian women. These resources taught me practical ways to be a godly wife and mother. Ultimately, how to be a godly woman. I strongly feel that they became my mentors and friends, and I am so grateful that they took the time to pen some powerful books.

As I was learning and growing, God gave me opportunities to mentor women as they began their journey in homeschooling. I started the W.O.W. (Women of Worth) ministry at church. It was and still is my heart's desire to help women develop in four top areas of their lives, the four W's: Word and Worship, Wisdom in Relationships, Wealth Management, and Wellness.

All throughout my life, I heard people's stories. Their cries for acceptance, approval and significance. As families came to our church, David and I loved on them. We knew they were searching for answers and though we did not have all the answers we knew who did, God. We saw lives being transformed, healings and manifestations of God's goodness and mercy. We were awestruck.

Slowly, I began to see how the pieces of my life were falling into place. As a child, I had a desire to become a missionary and teach people about God. In my mind, I thought that would mean living in some remote village, and I was willing to do that. But, God brought me to the States, the land of "milk and honey," the land of plenty of churches. How in the world was I supposed to be a missionary here?

As I write this, I am reminded of a certain day in my life. It was one morning, I am not sure where I was going, but I was driving, and I had the radio tuned to Moody Bible Broadcast. I liked listening to several of the teachings, and one of my favorites was Chuck Swindoll's series on Moses. I can't remember the particular teaching that day, but what I do know was that I was pulling off to the side of the road and just weeping. I sat there for a few minutes trying to regain my composure and soak in what I had just heard. It wasn't Chuck Swindoll's voice I heard that morning; it was God's voice. God was telling me that He had called me to be a type of "Moses" to women. He wanted me to help deliver them out of their bondages and teach them how to be free in Him. He wanted me to be an example to women of how godly women should conduct themselves and live. I was overwhelmed. And I responded in the same way that Moses did. *"Not me, God, you have the wrong person. I am not good at speaking. I am terrified of speaking in front of people."* I had to get over myself and my inadequacies. This was not about me; it was about God.

This was my clarion missionary call! I was created and born for this reason.

This was my clarion missionary call! I was created and born for this reason. I see now how God has brought me to a place where I can be an ambassador for Him. That means I represent Christ on this earth. I am His hands and feet. As a pastor's wife, I have been given the honor and privilege to serve the people in our church. I am humbled and do not take this role lightly or for granted in any way. When I put together a meal for someone who is sick or just had a baby, I am showing the love of Christ. When I sit with someone at the hospital, I am showing the love of Christ. When I pray for someone or send them a card, I am showing the love of Christ. When I teach the children at children's church, I am telling them about God. When I love my husband and take care of him, I am setting an example and being a role model. It is possible to have a fulfilled, and beautiful marriage. When I train up my children in the way that they should go, I am helping others to see that it is possible to raise godly children in an ungodly world.

I am reminded of the story in the Bible, after the resurrection, Jesus appeared to His disciples, and Thomas was not there at that gathering. Jesus left, Thomas came in, and all the disciples were telling him what had taken place; they had just seen Jesus. Thomas did not believe them; he said he needed to put his hands in the nail-pierced hands of Jesus and place his hand in Jesus' side to believe. We laugh and call him Doubting Thomas, but I believe many are saying the same thing today. They know God, love God and believe in God, but they want to see Him. As believers, it is our responsibility to show Jesus to everyone.

I shared a snapshot of my life so you can get to know me. I trust and pray that you will see my heart and my desire for you to become a noble woman. It is possible; you can become a woman of distinction. You can rise above the norm and be a woman of excellence. It is never too late!

I have laid out seven pillars you can establish in your life. Take these principles, apply the practical steps, and see yourself grow into the noble woman God created you to be. You will experience God's peace and gain an understanding of His purpose for your life. You don't have just to survive life; you can thrive and live life to the fullest. Jesus said, *". . . I came that they may have life, and have it abundantly" (John 10:10b)*

Introduction

We don't hear the word noble used these days very much, and if you do, it seldom refers to a noble woman or man. That kind of language belonged in medieval times, where men or women were regarded as noble based upon their rank or title. The only way to become noble back in that period was by birth or by marriage. It was a respected title with an elevated lifestyle.

The word noble is associated with more than just a period or era. It is related to who you and I are. We are noble women. What makes us noble, you ask? Our Heavenly Father is a King, and anyone who is a part of His family is automatically, without question, given the rightful position of nobility. We are heirs together with Jesus Christ.

This book is not about convincing you that you are noble. You simply have to embrace and accept that truth. This book is about fulfilling our calling as noble women so that we can become women of distinction. Women who are set apart, governing their lives by principles, and order. Women who have beaten the odds and have risen far above the norm.

In the book of Ruth, Boaz says to Ruth, "And now, my daughter, don't be afraid. I will do for you all you ask. All the people of my town know that you are a woman of noble character" (Ruth 3:11 NIV).

Ruth was a stranger in Naomi's town, but she managed to gain the respect and honor of the city by her character of nobility. What about you, my dear sister, don't you want to be known and defined as a woman of noble character? Your noble character will give you access and favor.

Join me on this journey as we discover the seven pillars of truth. Seven is a Biblical number equated with completeness. It is my desire that these seven truth pillars will help you to become complete as a noble woman. A true mark and making of a woman of distinction.

At the end of each chapter, you will find *Points to Ponder,* a snapshot summary of the highlights. I have included *Proclamations,* power statements to declare and keep you grounded. And *Personal Reflection* questions to help you do some soul searching to guide you in your pursuit of becoming a noble woman.

I chose the word pillars because they are a symbol of strength and endurance. Regardless of what storms or life challenges may come our way, nothing should be able to shake our pillars of truth. These are God's truths, and they should remain permanent in our lives.

Again, going back to the ancient times many buildings and structures were built with pillars. In some situations, natural disasters have destroyed buildings, but the pillars have remained. Proverbs 9:1 (NIV) says, "Wisdom hath built her house; she has set up its seven pillars:"

In the book of Proverbs, wisdom is personified as a woman. So, could it be that a noble or wise woman can build her house or life by establishing seven pillars? And let's go one step further, by developing these seven pillars she can experience wholeness, completeness, and order in her life and home.

My dear sisters, let us be the generation that rises to live wholeheartedly and intentionally the way that God designed us to live. We owe it to ourselves, to our families, our children and most importantly to God.

"True womanhood is a distinctive calling of God to display the glory of His Son in ways that could not be displayed if there were not womanhood." *John Piper*

We must not lose the essence of femininity. The qualities of gentleness, tenderness, sensitivity and a spirit that nurtures, these traits were given to us by God. Let us embrace who we were created to be. It's time to rediscover our original design and live up to our God-given calling.

Pillar I - The Pattern

"You are not a product of your past, but of an original pattern." Sylvia Banks

Why does it seem so much easier to remember the bad and forget the good? To assume the worst, rather than believe the best? Could it be that we have allowed our minds to be hard-wired to a pattern of negativity that is wrong? Rather than search for the truth and discover our original design, we have settled to buy a bag of lies, and it has cost us everything!

Now here we stand at the crossroads of life, and we wonder: Who am I? What do I have and where am I going? You see, I need to go back to the day you were born. Every child that enters this world comes not only with wrinkled skin, a set of lungs, and a hearty appetite but also with three essential questions. They are: Who am I? Am I loved? Do I have significance? Unfortunately, for many, these crucial questions go unanswered, and as these children grow up, they meander through life seeking answers to these questions. They fall prey to the world and the systems of the world that falsely attempt to answer these questions. The results are that they are left more empty, more lonely, and more depressed than before, so the vicious cycle continues. It is a cyclical pattern going from relationship to relationship, job to job, and circumstance to circumstance because there is a longing inside for these three fundamental questions to be answered.

> We have settled to buy a bag of lies, and it has cost us everything!

Where does one go? What does one do? Who will answer these questions? God in His infinite grace and mercy had it all planned out from the very beginning. He knew this would happen so He gave us an insurance-assurance policy. No deductibles to meet, no co-pays, and no out-of-pocket expenses. He wanted you and me to be completely assured of who we are, that we are loved, and that we have significance. In His Word, God defines how He created us, and who He created us to be.

Original Design

It is time to understand your original design. When God created you, He had a thought and then a vision to see His thought come to pass, and the result is YOU! An original is something that is new, inventive, and created for the first time. Design means to form or conceive an idea in the mind to intend for a definite purpose.

You may have read in Genesis 2:21, that God caused a deep sleep to fall upon man and He took one of his ribs, closed up that place, and *fashioned* into a woman the rib which He had taken from man. The word *fashioned* here means that He took the time to build or create the woman. He created you from an original thought because He had a purpose for you to fulfill.

Jeremiah 29:11 says: "For I know the plans that I have for you," declares the Lord, "plans for welfare and not for calamity to give you a future and hope."

Perhaps you have formulated your identity, that is, who you are, from your past, people's opinions, performance (the way you have been able to do things), or from your present situation. We cannot deny these events in our life, and they have played a part in shaping who we are today, but where the truth gets twisted is that we have used these events to define and describe who we are.

I am ___________________ because this is what
my ______________ told me.

(You fill in the blanks. What have you labeled yourself? Who gave you that label?)

This thought process leads one to have a

negative perception of one's self. The events in your life become stumbling blocks instead of stepping stones to your life of purpose and fulfillment. How can you believe that God has plans for you that are wonderful and a future that is bursting with opportunities?

It is a step of faith to erase and eradicate misconceptions of who you are; it leaves you feeling rather naked and vulnerable. What and who are you without these labels and tags that have identified who you are for so long? In a way, they have become your "comfort zone" labels because it allows you to give excuses to stay in your rut.

My dear sister, God, never designed or desired for you to live your life in this way. He provided a way for you to experience life to the fullest. He wants you to rise beyond your circumstances and live a life of purpose. Please don't misunderstand, struggles will be a part of our lives, but life itself was not intended to be a struggle.

We can never fully grasp the magnitude of our original design; it is so much bigger than our finite minds can comprehend. Original design is valuable, unique, and priceless. Why do you think original artifacts and paintings are kept in museums? Some are enclosed in glass boxes. It is because of their value. An original will not be reproduced again. You can purchase a copy of an original painting, and though it is beautiful, it is still not the original.

I've looked around my house for original artifacts and works of art, and it appears that everything that I have purchased from the paintings and wall decorations are copies of an original. Now there are a couple of things hanging on my wall that happens to be original works of art. They are paintings and signs that I have created. These are original works of art, and you won't find a duplicate of these anywhere. I know the value of these items, not in a monetary sense but the fact that it took time and effort. They may not be your Picasso or Rembrandt, but they are unique, and they tell a story.

> God created you after a pattern, and that pattern was Himself.

What about when you look at yourself? Can you see that you are an original work of art? God created you with all your gifts and talents and placed those inside of you so that you could use them. There is no one on this earth like you. You are unique, valuable, and therefore priceless. You must value your life because God does. He is the master designer who created you with a purpose and for His glory.

I've signed and dated my works of art, and I am proud of what I have been able to do. These pieces of art started out with a thought, and then a vision, and finally a completed masterpiece. Our master designer, God, operated in the same manner when

He created each of us. He had a thought, and then a vision, and finally a completed masterpiece. You are His masterpiece.

God writes to us in Genesis 1:27: "And God created man in His own image, in the image of God He created him, male and female He created them." So what does this mean? God created you after a pattern, and that pattern was Himself. We were created in His image, which means likeness. We resemble God. All the attributes that are a part of God's character and nature are also residing in us. Yes, it's hard to believe when we see the way some people live and act. It is far from the resemblance of God.

But, this is my challenge to you. Are you willing to go back to the pattern and resemble God? It means changing your way of thinking to His way of thinking, your way of doing and being to His way. Seems impossible, doesn't it, especially when you have been conditioned to have a negative way of thinking and your actions and attitudes have reflected that. However, God tells us in His assurance plan that *"nothing is impossible with God."* You see, there's the assurance, with God's help we can make the necessary changes to our lives. He promises to help us if we allow Him to.

I love how the psalmist, David, captured his heart's cry to God in Psalm 51:10-13: "Create in me a clean heart, O God, and renew a steadfast spirit within me. Do not cast me away from Your presence and do not take Your Holy Spirit from me. Restore to me the joy of Your salvation and sustain me with a willing spirit."

If a king can humble himself and make it his heart's cry and prayer to ask God to clean his heart and renew him, then you can, too. King David had committed some major crimes at this point in his life, but he was willing to own up to his mistakes, face the consequences, and seek God's forgiveness. God was faithful to forgive him and restore him back to the original pattern. The Bible tells us that God references David as a *"man after His own heart."* That should tell you what a loving and merciful God we have.

Value of the Pattern

I've mentioned the word, *"pattern,"* so let's take a moment to explore this word and bring some clarity. One of the definitions that the dictionary gives is, *"an original model considered for or deserving of imitation."*

I've sewn a few things in my lifetime, and every time I have attempted to do so, I have used a pattern. The pattern is the original design, and whatever I created using that pattern is an imitation of that pattern. Now, I have the freedom to be creative and add various embellishments to give it some uniqueness, but still, I have used an original design to create my masterpiece.

This information may be a lot to take in right

now, and you may need some time to chew on this truth. God is the original design, and we are patterned after Him. We each have our uniqueness, personality, and character, but we still resemble our original design. We were created to be His representatives on this earth. God is in heaven; we are on this earth as His ambassadors. We represent our King and Master.

When people see you, can they also see God? Do you reflect His image? Do you bear His name? Everything we say or do should be an extension of who God is. If He is truly living in us, then we should also be allowing Him to flow through us.

Perhaps you are questioning God's love for you. You might be asking how can God love me? Let me illustrate it this way. Just imagine that a friend has asked you for a twenty-dollar bill. You give this to your friend, and she takes it and balls it up and throws in on the ground. She proceeds to stomp on the twenty-dollar bill, all the while telling it that it is nothing and that it is worthless. This scene goes on for a few seconds. She picks up the crumpled bill and returns it to you and walks away. In your shock and disbelief, you look at the bill and smooth out the wrinkles. Now, tell me, has the value of the bill changed? It underwent some abuse. But the value of the bill has not changed. Any way you look at it, it is still a twenty-dollar bill. You can take it to the bank or use it at the store. What no one will deny is that it is still a twenty-dollar bill.

I use this illustration, painting a picture for you

of your value. Before you were even born, God deemed you as valuable. Psalm 139:13-16 says: "For You formed my inward parts; You wove me in my mother's womb. I will give thanks to You, for I am fearfully and wonderfully made; wonderful are your works, and my soul knows it very well. My frame was not hidden from You when I was made in secret, and skillfully wrought in the depths of the earth; Your eyes have seen my unformed substance; and in Your book were written the days that were ordained for me, when as yet there was not one of them."

How powerful to know that God saw you while you were formed and before you were even born He wrote your life story. He is omniscient, so He knew everything that would happen to you and everything that you would do. And yet; still, He loves you, values you, and has a plan for your life. Don't question His love for you; receive it and in return obey Him by choosing to mirror His image/pattern in your life.

Close the Door to the Past

The past is a culmination of events, life experiences, tragedies and joys that have all taken place in your life. There are some wonderful memories to treasure and people to remember. There are victories and milestones to celebrate. However, life is not always rosy; there are pains, disappointments, shame and guilt that pose as skeletons, haunting and daunting you.

Let me tell you; the enemy would love to keep you in a cocoon of your past. In a cocoon, you are all alone with yourself. That's right, self-pity, self-doubt, low self-esteem, and no self-confidence or self-image. The word that I see repeated here is: "self." The cocoon may serve as a protective covering for a short while, but at some point, you are going to have to break out of the cocoon. The longer you stay inside the cocoon, the more self-centered, self-conscious, and selfish you will become. These words do not describe a noble woman; she is far from being a self-centered individual. She is selfless-not in the sense that she totally loses herself and becomes a "nobody," but in the sense that she does not have to be concerned with herself and the day-to-day dealings of life. She trusts in her master designer, God, who has promised to take care of her and meet her every need. Therefore, she is free to look to the world around her and serve those in need, whether it is her family or an unfamiliar face, she gives selflessly of her time, gifts and talents.

> You have a purpose and destiny!

Breaking out of the cocoon means bringing closure to the past. I realize you may have endured some very painful experiences, losses, and violations. My heart breaks for you, and I pray that you can release the past to pursue your future. It is not easy to forgive those who have hurt you. It's not easy to let go of the pain when you see the scars that remind you daily of what was in the past. My dear sister, it is time to face the truth and be set free from what is damaging you. You have a purpose and destiny. Don't let the enemy steal the future from you. He might have stolen your past, but don't allow him to steal what God has promised you.

Have you ever considered what would happen if a larvae remained larvae? It would never grow into a caterpillar and emerge into a beautiful butterfly. It is a growth process, and you probably studied that in science class. It's called the life cycle. Coming out of your cocoon may not feel comfortable, but it is the first step in moving forward. Then just like the caterpillar, you will become that beautiful butterfly. Imagine what our world would be like without butterflies. As a child, I loved to catch butterflies and look at their beautiful wings. The designs and colors were so intricately created. Only a master designer could have created such original insects. And did you know they have a purpose? They fly around from flower to flower to gather pollen and spread that pollen to help produce beautiful flowers all around the world.

God is faithful to use even the ugly things in our lives for our good and His glory. I urge you to do whatever it takes to close the door of your past. Don't be a slave to it. If you need to seek professional counseling, then do it. If you need to talk to your pastor or pastor's wife, then do it. If you just need to pray and ask God to help you, then do it. He is waiting for you, and He will move on your behalf, but you have to give Him access to enter into your heart and give Him full control of your life.

Are you ready to commit your life and heart to God? I want to invite you into the Kingdom of God to meet the master designer of life. If you have never done this before, then I encourage you to pray this prayer. Perhaps it has been a long time since you prayed this prayer and you have drifted from God. Let me ask you also to recommit your life to God and pray this prayer again.

Heavenly Father,

I admit that I am a sinner. I acknowledge that I need you as my personal Savior. I believe you sent your begotten Son, Jesus, on this earth to die for me. You have cleansed me from my sins, the past, present, and future. I believe that Jesus died on the cross and rose again from the grave. Therefore, I receive the gift of eternal life. I confess and proclaim that Jesus is Lord of my life. Amen

Welcome to the family of God, my dear precious sister. I may never meet you here on earth, but I know we will be together in heaven.

By praying this prayer, you have given God permission to have complete control of your life. You have promised to surrender your will to His will. The slate has been wiped clean for you, and you are now born-again. You are a new creation in Christ Jesus. The old is gone, and the new has come.

"Therefore, if anyone is in Christ, he is a new creature; the old things passed away; behold, new things have come" (Corinthians 5:17).

"He doesn't treat us as our sins deserve, nor pay us back in full for our wrongs. As high as heaven is over the earth, so strong is his love to those who fear him. And as far as sunrise is from sunset, he has separated us from our sins" (Psalm 103:10-12 MSG).

Are you getting the picture now of what a loving God and Abba, Father we have? He never turned His back on you; He was just waiting for you to invite Him to be a part of your life. Remember this; your past is a testimony of where you have been, not where you are going!

Close the door to the past once and for all. Forgive those who have hurt you and forgive yourself for mistakes you have made. Set yourself free to live, laugh, and love.

"To forgive is to set a prisoner free and discover that the prisoner was you."
Lewis Smedes.

Peace to Pursue Life

One of my favorite scriptures as a young girl was John 14: 14: "Peace I leave with you; my peace I give to you; not as the world gives do I give to you. Do not let your heart be troubled, do not let it be fearful." I grew up in Africa, and we endured some terrible political situations. I was in a boarding school away from my parents. We did not have the convenience of technology to stay in touch with each other. This beautiful promise from God was my lifeline during those trying times. I just knew I had to trust God to keep my family and me safe. And you know, He did!

There is nothing like having peace, God's peace. The word *shalom* is the Hebrew word for peace, and it means, nothing missing and nothing broken. You see when you understand that you are an original design, created from a pattern to emulate that pattern, you can have peace, knowing that you have been restored back to your original design. Your past has been taken care of and now there is nothing missing or broken, everything is intact again. You can move forward and be renewed and refreshed. No one can go too far with excess baggage. It is costly and weighs you down. It's time to travel light. Don't allow the things of this world to weigh you down.

Jesus spoke these words to His disciples in John 16:33: "These things I have spoken to you so that in me you may have peace. In the world you have tribulation, but take courage; I have overcome the world."

As a noble woman, remember your address is not here on this earth. You are a part of the Kingdom of God. You are here on an assignment to be His representative and ambassador. You have released the old, and you are embracing the new. Does this mean that you will not experience challenges or rough waters? Not! We live in a fallen world, and you don't have to look too far to see the destruction that is taking place around us. Things will happen, and your faith will be tried and tested again and again. God's assurance plan, however, tells us that we will have His peace even in the midst of trials and storms. There's no need to live in fear because He has overcome the world. The safest place to be is abiding in Him (John 15:4).

Know the Pattern and become the Pattern for others to follow!

Points to Ponder

- Understand your original design.
- You are valuable, unique, and whole.
- God created you in His likeness and image; you bear His image.
- Learn to become a reflection of the original design.
- Release the past.
- Embrace God's peace.

Proclamation

- I am an original design; there is no one else like me.
- I was created in the image of God; I bear His image.
- I will release the past and embrace His peace.
- I will be a reflection of the original pattern.

Personal Reflection

1. What memories or scars are you holding on to? Write them down in pencil. Take a last look at what you wrote; now erase them. That's exactly what God has promised to do for you. He is willing to remove your past.

2. Read Isaiah 43: 18-19, what a great promise. He wants to do something new in your life. Write a short prayer here, asking God to help you receive the new "thing" in your life.

3. God has created you as an original individual. What do you enjoy doing? What are your gifts and talents? Make a list of your talents.

4. Have you ever created something original? Perhaps it's a song, a poem, painting or craft. Challenge yourself and make or create something original. Feel free to use the blank pages provided as your creative space. I know you can do it!

CREATIVE SPACE

Pillar II - Purpose

"The greatest tragedy in life is not death, but a life without a purpose." Dr. Myles Munroe

From a simple straight pin to the largest excavating machine, everything created serves a purpose. You would not use your rice cooker to make a smoothie, and you certainly would not use your blender to cook your rice. When something is not used for what it is created, it cannot fulfill its purpose. Suppose, I purchased a blender and tried to cook rice in it. After several attempts, frustrated, I return the item to the store, and the cashier asks me to fill out a brief form explaining my reason for returning the blender. I proceed to write down that the blender does not work properly, and it will not cook my rice. The cashier looks at my explanation and proceeds to tell me that the blender was not designed to cook rice, only to blend items that I placed in the jar. You see the problem was not with the blender. I was not using it for its intended purpose.

It sounds a little funny and maybe even silly. But it does prove my point, everything has a purpose and should be used for the purpose it was created to produce the necessary results. Before a product is produced the manufacturer must determine its purpose, so in other words, the purpose must come before the product.

How does this relate to our lives? Let's take a look at the story of Esther. She was a young orphaned teenager who was being raised by a loving and caring relative, her cousin, Mordecai. We don't know all the details of her life but through a series of events, Esther was selected to be one of the young ladies who could be the queen of Persia. She kept her identity and heritage a secret as her cousin had instructed her. She was a very likable girl and quickly found favor with the people in the palace.

As it was the custom of the day, Esther, entered into a twelve-month period of preparation before she would even be summoned to see the king. She was being groomed with external oils and perfumes to enhance her outward beauty, but God was grooming her on the inside and building her character. When her turn came to meet the king, he was pleased with her and placed the crown on her head. She was now the new queen of Persia.

Mordecai kept in touch with Esther and informed her of the horrific plot to kill and destroy the Jewish people. Mordecai begged Esther to beseech the king to save her and her people. Esther declined and reminded Mordecai of the protocol and the risk of losing her life to make an appearance before the king without an invitation. Mordecai gave Esther a wake-up call and reminded her that just because she lived in a palace, she too was not safe. God would find someone to save his people. Then Mordecai asks this classic question, "Maybe you were made queen for just such a time as this?" (Esther 4:14 MSG)

Something stirred in Esther; her passion was now revealing her purpose.

Esther realized the solution to this problem was within her. She had a platform and had been strategically positioned. Now her task was to activate her purpose and developed a plan. Esther's passion for her people was worth risking her life.

Something stirred in Esther; her passion was now revealing her purpose. Esther, in all her noble beauty, made an immediate impact on the King. Again, Esther was keenly aware that the purpose she carried inside of her was not just for herself, but also for her nation. She had the power to preserve her people.

After arranging a dinner for the King and Haman, Esther revealed the plot to destroy her people. When the King inquired who was responsible for this plot, she pointed to Haman.

Esther's willingness to walk in her purpose caused the enemy of her people, Haman, to be defeated. Her courageous victory gave her an eternal place in Jewish history. Even today, the Feast of Purim is celebrated in honor of Queen Esther. (To read the full account of this wonderful true story, read the book of Esther.)

Our society puts considerable emphasis on performance. We are conditioned to focus on what we are going to do in life rather than on who we are going to become. Our educational system is grooming our children for what they are going to do in their lives, their careers, and their profession. Little training is given in shaping their purpose and who they are to become. It is an admirable accomplishment to obtain an education and degrees behind your name. There's nothing wrong with having a great job or career and being financially set, but what if you find yourself ultimately miserable doing the very thing you were trained and conditioned to do. Then, I dare say you are not fulfilling your purpose.

Please understand, I value education. We have been privileged to homeschool our three children, and during this process of educating them, we realized we needed to not only focus on their academics, but we also hone in on their purpose. We recognized their skills, talents, and abilities and challenged them to channel those passions towards their purpose. Ultimately, once you activate and cultivate purpose, it can become your profession. You will find fulfillment. It is your destiny to be "purpose-minded" rather than "performance-driven."

Realizing your purpose stirs a passion inside of you. It's what wakes you up and keeps you going. It's what brings meaning, direction, and a sense of fulfillment in your life. Your purpose can potentially solve a major crisis. Isn't that what Esther did? Just a poor little village orphan girl. She did not meet the qualifications to fulfill the position of a queen. The king was not seeking qualifications; he was only after beauty and someone who would not defy him. But, because Esther realized her purpose he received more than he was seeking. She operated in her purpose, and God's people were blessed. God is not looking for your qualifications, but rather your availability. He will qualify you if you make yourself available to Him. The way to make yourself available is to submit to His will and His way.

Discover Your Purpose

Dear friend, I hope this is encouraging to you. Esther is still celebrated today all over the world by Jews. I believe this story was intentionally recorded in the Bible to inspire us. It is a powerful reminder that regardless of your situation, God can and will use you. Sometimes, you have to be willing to risk everything. You have to understand that your purpose is not about you, but about what God can do through you.

Please understand your purpose is embedded inside of you. It is the blueprint of your life. The events in your life are a part of the journey to bring you to your purpose. Everything that happens is for preparation.

To assist you in discovering your purpose, I am going to include a tool that my husband designed. We have used this assessment many times. It has helped numerous people find their purpose. By using this tool, businesses have been birthed, books were written, ministries and organizations have been planted.

Follow the instructions and you will have a clear and concise purpose statement.

Personal Purpose Discovery Assessment

This tool is designed to help you discover the REAL you. You are not defined by what you have been through nor are you defined by how you or others view who you are because it could be a faulty perception.

Your purpose is the original intent for your existence. You were born with a purpose, and this is who God designed you to be.

What are the benefits of understanding your design?

- Produces order
- Properly used and not abused
- Perform at an optimum level
- Protect your purpose
- Pleases God, your creator

What results can I expect from understanding my purpose

- Position of leadership
- Productivity
- Provision
- Personal fulfillment
- Problem solver

Five Questions to Discover Your Purpose

1. What do you see in society that burdens or grieves you? (It may cause you to be either angry or sad).

2. What group of people are you passionate about? (Circle one)

☐ People in general	☐ Children	☐ Couples
☐ Professionals	☐ Adults	☐ Families
☐ Teens	☐ Women	☐ Singles
☐ Religious groups	☐ Non-Christians	☐ Seniors
☐ An ethnic group	☐ Men	
☐ Single family households	☐ Other____________	

3. What would be your message to this group? (What's your objective? What do you want to accomplish with this group?)

4. Choose words of how you would like to help this group (circle two).

☐ Create	☐ Lead	☐ Nurture
☐ Discover	☐ Empower	☐ Impart
☐ Teach	☐ Influence	☐ Repair
☐ Encourage	☐ Impact	☐ Challenge
☐ Comfort	☐ Develop	☐ Support
☐ Serve	☐ Revive	☐ Renew
☐ Change	☐ Equip	☐ Motivate
☐ Coach	☐ Organize	☐ Counsel

☐ Other______________________

5. What do you want this group to become as a result of your influence?

Examples:

To live successful lives
To be productive
Maximize their potential
To obtain more out of their lives

To reach higher goals
To enjoy their life
Other_______________

The Purpose Code

Take the answers to the questions and follow the CODE: 4,2,3,5. Write down what you wrote for each of the five questions.

#4

#2

#3

#5

Example: *To motivate and empower people to discover their purpose and potential to* live fulfilling lives.

My purpose is:

You have just discovered your purpose. Congratulations! We established earlier that everyone was born with a purpose, and this is their *blueprint.* Each person was given a unique reason for being on this earth, and that is their *fingerprint.* Now, you can find out what field you are to impact, and that will be your *footprint.*

Find Your Field to Impact and Leave a Footprint

- ☐ Home
- ☐ Education
- ☐ Medical
- ☐ Ministry
- ☐ Business
- ☐ Government
- ☐ Arts (Media, Technology, Music)
- ☐ Land/Community

Manage Your Purpose

As we walked through the story of Esther, we saw how valuable it was for her to know her purpose. Knowing your purpose is like having a *blueprint* for your life. It's an overview or outline so that you can develop a plan of action. It guides you in your course of life.

God has given us a universal blueprint in His Word that we as believers must adhere. These are guidelines and standards set in place for us to follow. As we follow these guidelines, we can experience successes and triumphs in our life. We are not exempt from situations and circumstances that at times can be painful and devastating. The great news, however, is that we have a blueprint that guides us, allowing us to know how to respond to our life experiences.

What you just discovered as you followed the instructions to the *Purpose Discovery* assessment is your individual purpose. It is your *fingerprint.* Not only do we have a collective purpose, but we also each have our individual purpose to live out. You have been given an active part to play in His Kingdom.

You might be thinking, "How am I going to accomplish this?" You are right; your purpose statement is going to be bigger than you. Why? It is because the God that lives inside of you is larger than you. There's also something very exciting to know that God desires to use you to fulfill His purpose on this earth. You are an intricate part of His grand plan.

I have taken this assessment on several occasions in various settings. I have noticed that though the wording may slightly change, the premise of my purpose has never changed. My purpose is to help women; it is my passion. My purpose statement reads like this, *To teach and encourage women to rise above the norm and pursue excellence in every area of their lives.*

At the time I discovered my purpose, we had just planted a church. I was beginning my journey as a homeschool mom and had many hats to wear. I wondered where I would find the time to teach and encourage women. I was passionate about it, but I certainly did not know how to go about it.

Well, whenever in doubt, the best thing to do is pray. Esther did the same thing. She along with her Jewish brothers and sisters spent time in prayer expecting God to reveal the plan to them. I had to do the same thing. I prayed and asked God to show me what He wanted me to do. I made myself available for His service.

It is comforting to know that God will never ask us to do anything that we cannot handle. He knows the seasons of our life. God also equips us to do the things He wants us to do. He has promised that He will NEVER leave us nor forsake us. That means He will be with us always.

I am reminded of a little gift that a friend of mine gave me in high school. It was a little ceramic jewelry box. There was nothing fancy about it, but the inscription on the box will forever be etched in my heart. It said, *"Great occasions for serving God come seldom, but little ones surround us daily." St. Francis de Sales*

In a nutshell, that short, powerful sentence sums it all up. Every day we have opportunities to impact someone's life. As I mentioned previously, for me, it was the little things, like taking a meal to someone. I enjoy cooking, and I cook for my family every day and still do. It just takes a little extra effort to make a little extra to share. I discovered the talents and abilities God had given me could be used to serve Him and serve my purpose. It all fit together, like puzzle pieces creating a picture. Serving my purpose is not a drudgery, it fuels me, and I am so blessed and energized after every small endeavor.

I want to encourage you to look carefully at the wording of your purpose statement. You may want to write it out on notecards and place it in various locations as a daily reminder. Memorize and recite it; allow your purpose to become you.

As your purpose becomes you, opportunities will arise for you to serve your purpose. Perhaps, it's a speaking engagement, an opportunity to showcase your talent or share your testimony. The possibilities are endless. A lady I know would spend time at the homeless shelter for women. She would take the time to talk with them, encourage them and just be their friend. Having had a tough life herself, she was able to relate to their situations, and she was also able to give them hope.

> You have been given an active part to play in His Kingdom.

Keep a notepad or use modern technology to keep track of creative ideas God will provide you with. Maybe you have a passion for teenage girls. You could invite these girls to come to your house, spend time with them, love them, and provide a haven for them. It doesn't take much. A little bit of time, effort and investment go a long way. There's a lady in our church who loves kids. She is a make-up artist. So, just imagine girls and make-up. She invites young girls to her home, and as she applies external make-up on them to make them look beautiful, she also explains to them that real beauty lies within them. How powerful and what an impact this will make on any teenage girl.

Every little thing you do for someone else matters to God. You are extending His arms of love,

His eyes that say, "I care," and His feet that are willing to go the extra mile. Your purpose may solve a problem; it may serve a need, but it will always serve others. And in serving others, you are ultimately serving God. It will make an impact and a difference in someone else's life. This intentional style of living gives purpose to everything you do.

Discover your purpose, live it and share it!

Points to Ponder

- You were created for a purpose
- Your purpose is embedded inside of you
- It is up to you to discover your purpose
- Your passion will reveal your purpose
- Your purpose will bring fulfillment

Proclamation

- I have a purpose
- I was created or God's purpose and glory
- My purpose gives me the reason for my existence
- My passion is a part of my purpose
- My purpose will help me to live intentionally
- I can maximize my potential by knowing my purpose

PERSONAL REFLECTION

1. You should have completed your Purpose Discovery Assessment. How do you feel now that you have discovered your purpose? Do you see how it fits in with who you are?

2. Make a list of places and ways you can use your purpose. Maybe you are an encourager; you could start a blog. Perhaps you could volunteer at a nursing home if you feel called to help the elderly. Small acts of kindness do make remarkable impacts.

3. Do you know someone that could benefit from discovering their purpose? Visit the website: noblewoman.net to obtain more copies of this tool.

Pillar III - Principles

"Be sure you put your feet in the right place, and then stand firm." Abraham Lincoln

The word principle comes from a Latin word. It means *the cause, source, or origin of anything. It also expresses to establish firmly in the mind, the beliefs that influence your actions.*

According to Stephen Covey, "The choice of purpose represents our destination. The choice for principles then determines the means for how we will get there—how we will attain our goals."

As noble women, who are representatives of the King of Kings, it is imperative that we govern our lives by principles. Without principles in our lives, we will fall for everything and stand for nothing.

In the world that we live in the focus is on freedom rather than principle. The messages conveyed to us through the media, our peers, and publications are all inviting us to live freely. Live for the moment, do what you want to do when you want to do it. There are no rules, just live. I recall this statement that Dr. Tony Evans made during a radio broadcast, "Freedom is not doing what you want, but doing what you ought."

Unfortunately, living a life without principles, guidelines, or standards is an invitation to a life of problems. The decisions you make will be feeling driven. Our feelings are not constant; they are forever changing. Our feelings and emotions can lead us into trouble.

We are emotional beings, and God created us with our feelings, but they were never designed to guide us. Our emotions are an expression of our feelings, good or bad. Of course, there are appropriate ways to express our emotions. It takes maturity and self-control.

There is a way in which a noble woman chooses to live her life. The key word here is, chooses. It is a choice. However, if you have decided to make Jesus your Lord and Savior and He is now the King of your life, then you have willfully chosen to surrender your will for God's will.

If you are a parent, you know the importance of establishing principles in your home. Your children need and require guidelines to navigate their lives. It will help them to become responsible. They also need principles to guide them in making choices and decisions in their lives.

The words boundaries, rules, and guidelines can sound restrictive. These words are not popular in today's culture. And therefore, they are the very building blocks that are lacking in today's culture. We can read and see what the absence of these elements has done to our society. There is far too much chaos and mayhem.

Three Principles

Learn to embrace principles and live by them. Boundaries give us parameters for freedom. Here are three principles that you can start implementing in your life.

1. **Discipline**-is a system of order. Discipline has to begin with you. You have to take the steps for personal discipline in your life. You need to establish a system of order for every day of your life. Create a routine. It doesn't matter whether you are a stay-at-home mom, a business owner, or a working woman. Establishing order in your life will minimize chaos and distractions. You will have a plan in place to follow.

Creating a system of order will also help you to manage life efficiently when unexpected emergencies or last minute changes happen. Instead of falling apart or feeling overwhelmed, you will be able to make wise decisions.

Some of the areas that we need to become more disciplined in are how much time we spend on electronics, watching TV, social media, and what we are feeding our body. It requires discipline to know when to unplug. It takes discipline to be able to stop eating after enjoying a few bites of a delicious brownie. It's all about moderation.

2. Discernment- is distinguishing between what is going to be beneficial or detrimental to you. For my dear sisters that are single, please understand that you have to have discernment when it comes to relationships. You are going to have to go beyond what he looks like and what he drives. Think and ask some questions. What is his work ethic? How does he manage his money? What is his character? How does he treat others? What do his friends say about him? Most importantly, what is his relationship with God? Does he have a relationship with God?

I have come across too many single women who have compromised their standards and ignored the red flags. The book of Proverbs talks about the foolish woman. Please do not be foolish; use wise judgment. If things are not adding up, there very well could be a reason for that. Don't turn a blind eye to what you see and a deaf ear to what you hear. A noble woman of value will attract a man of noble character and valor. But do be aware of the counterfeits. There are wolves dressed in sheep's clothing. The Bible warns about such men, so don't be so easily deceived or fooled. Take a step back, and look at the relationship from all angles.

A scripture I often share with single ladies is, "Many a man proclaims his own steadfast love, but a faithful man who can find?" (Proverbs 20:6 ESV) In other words, don't be swept away by flattering words. Does he have the mark and makings of a man who is loyal, trustworthy, and truthful?

Don't buy into the lie that you can change him after you get married. The chances are that whatever his character flaws are now, they will only be magnified later. You do not have the power to change anyone. You have the authority to influence him, but there are no guarantees for that change to take place.

God has given us the gift of discernment, and it is to be used to our advantage. As a wife, mother, and just as a woman, we will face decisions to make. Johnny may ask you if he can play at Tommy's house. Perhaps the atmosphere at Tommy's house is not a healthy one. As a mom, you are going to have to make a decision. Maybe you can suggest that Tommy comes over to your house.

As a noble woman, there will be many opportunities to use discernment. You may have business decisions to make. The way you manage the family finances will require judgment. How you relate to people will also be a matter of wisdom.

An intelligent woman is a wise woman. She realizes the decisions she makes today will affect her future, her family, her community, and her sphere of influence. It means she thinks before she acts, thinks before speaking, and thinks before she makes major decisions.

The key to discernment is maintaining an active prayer life. An intelligent woman is one who is seeking God's heart. She is in constant communication with her Heavenly Father because she has a personal relationship with Him. She relies on the Holy Spirit to guide her and give her counsel. A discerning woman makes decisions based on the principles in the Bible, not on her emotions. Proverbs 31:30 says, "But a woman who fears the Lord, she shall be praised." Here is the secret to her success, she fears the Lord, meaning she reverences, respects, and is in awe of Him. She is aware of her human frailty and the necessity for the sovereignty of God to guide her.

A wise, noble woman will choose her friends wisely. She will surround herself with ladies who have her best interest at heart. Women who will pray, encourage her in her roles of being a wife, mother, and a godly woman.

Steer clear from those who are negative and speak negatively to you and about you. Stay away from those who want to know your "business" and share everyone else's "business" with you. Gossip, backbiting, and slandering-none of these qualities are becoming of a noble woman.

Instead, be intentional and choose to use these two key guidelines in your speech from Proverbs 31: 26 "She opens her mouth in

wisdom, and the teaching of **kindness** is on her tongue." Dear friend, you can change the atmosphere in your home, workplace, and even church when you make it your goal for wisdom and kindness to flow out of your mouth.

3. Dignity-is honor and respect. You cannot expect others to respect you when you don't respect yourself. Hold yourself in high regard, not in a sense of pride, but in a sense of knowing who you are and being worthy of who you are. Proverbs 31:25 says, "Strength and dignity are her clothing, and she smiles at the future."

Strength is an everyday outfit for the noble woman.

These qualities are a beautiful portrait of a noble woman. It's not about a pretty face, the latest fashion, or outward adornment. Rather, it is the way that she dresses inwardly. She adorns herself with the qualities of godly character.

The word dignity in the Hebrew language means "splendor." Her splendor and regality come from a wardrobe that will never be out of style. She wears it gracefully and elegantly. I invite you, dear sister, to declutter your wardrobe. What's hanging in there that does not portray godly character? Discard those ugly attitudes, behaviors, and characteristics that mar splendor and majesty. You know what they are!

Strength is an everyday outfit for the noble

woman. She is strong physically because she takes care of herself. She has tremendous endurance and stamina. She is a smart worker. She knows her strengths and her limitations.

She also has a powerful mind. She is not a worrier but rather a warrior. She is prepared for the future. She has done well to take care of her finances. She has been trustworthy, spending, saving, and investing wisely. She is not concerned about the future, because when the time comes, her money will work for her.

For years, I did not want anything to do with our family finances. I was content to know how much to spend on groceries and content with a little pocket money. Math was not a strong subject for me, and so numbers only scared me. It seemed like an overwhelming responsibility, and I did not want to mess anything up.

My husband was doing a great job with the finances, but as the ministry was growing and opportunities were arising for him to travel and teach, I realized as his helpmate, it was time for me to step in.

I started with a little steno notebook and pen. I began keeping track of the incoming bills and put together a handmade calendar to schedule when the bills were due. It was a simple strategy, but it worked. It has been a tremendous help to my husband for me to oversee the finances. We work together on setting our goals and planning for the future. Finances in marriage can be a very sensitive issue. It is so important for a husband and wife to partner together in this area.

As a noble woman, you have to be able to be teachable. It is never too late to learn. Be willing to learn. As they say, "Knowledge is power." We recently participated in Dave Ramsey's *Financial Peace* course offered at our church. My husband and I didn't have to attend the course. Also, being the pastor and the pastor's wife, we could have said we know everything. But you know what, we were willing to learn. We are so thankful for the nuggets that we gleaned. We could see areas that we were right on track, and that was refreshing confirmation. Then we realized there were areas that we had not yet explored. We put into practice the information we received. We noticed positive changes in our finances. Learn to be a student; you can always learn something new.

We covered three important principles. I pray that you will embrace each of these principles and implement them in your daily life. It may seem like too much. I encourage you to start with one small step. Decide one discipline you want to incorporate in your life. Perhaps, you want to carve out a specific time to meet with God every day. Mark that on your calendar, and then be intentional about keeping that appointment. Start out with 10-15 minutes a day. Come prepared to talk to Him and also to listen to Him. Bring a journal and pen ready to write the "*downloads*" He gives you. He will be there on time waiting for you. As you become consistent, you can increase the time. To fulfill your goals, you need to make them achievable. Taking little steps towards your goal will enable you to see progress. Setting the bar too high will discourage you.

The Power of the Mind

The gentleman at the other end of the telephone line was telling me that there was a warrant out for my arrest and that the police would be on my doorstep the next morning to handcuff me and take me to jail. Being a law abiding citizen, a faithful taxpayer without a criminal record of any sort, I was totally caught off guard.

In my mind, I could already see the headline news for the newspaper, *"Pastor's Wife Arrested for Fraud against the IRS."* I saw all the photographs and the breaking news on all the TV channels. Yes, for a moment I saw it all and panicked! What would this do to our ministry, my husband, and children?

Now that I have your attention let me briefly explain. This incident happened to me, actually this week. I received a phone call from someone who identified himself from the IRS and even boldly gave me his badge number. He proceeded to inform me that the IRS was looking for me. My taxes did not match the IRS, and I owed several thousand dollars in back taxes. He informed me that our accountant had also been arrested. To settle the matter, I was to go to the local office supply store and file an electronic payment that very evening and the issue would be resolved.

After the fear factor, I shifted to the truth. As far as I know, we are in good standing with the IRS. We have a great accountant who takes care of all our taxes and runs a business of integrity. I realized there was no way this could even be true. The whole business about going to the office supply store sounded a bit odd, too. So, I disconnected the call.

Just to make sure that the call was indeed a fraudulent call, I called the accountant's office. The secretary picked up the phone and said he was out of the office. Could he possibly be in jail, I wondered? She must have sensed something in my tone, so she offered to help me. I explained the call I had just received, and she told me to ignore the matter. She informed me that the IRS never makes such phone calls. All their communication is through mail. I felt a little better, but still, I had to be sure. So I called the office supply store to see if they had some electronic device that could send money to the IRS. The kind man was probably laughing, but he assuredly told me that they did not have anything like that. Again I felt better, but still not quite convinced. I googled the number that I received the call from and saw that it indeed was a scam call. In fact, others had commented about receiving such calls of threat. Needless to say, I was totally relieved. (By the way, I was perturbed that such a phone call could have caused me to clean out our bank account. I did indeed report this to the IRS. I thought, let's see who gets arrested now.)

The point of sharing this crazy little scenario is to share with you how powerful our minds are. It can take us to places, create wild imaginations, and literally can transform us. That is the power of the mind.

Here are a few quotes about the mind from some well-known people. They, too, understood the impact our thoughts can have on us.

"If you think you can do a thing, or think you can't do a thing, you are right."-Henry Ford

"The world we have created is a product of our thinking; it cannot be changed without changing our thinking." -Albert Einstein

"A man is but the product of his thoughts. What he thinks, he becomes." –M. Gandhi

"Whatever the mind can conceive and believe, the mind can achieve." –Napoleon Hill

The enemy has been messing with our minds, our thoughts, for centuries. He gives us just enough information to cause us to doubt and to be deceived. Isn't that what happened to Eve in the Garden of Eden? God had given both Adam and Eve specific instructions as to what fruit tree they were not to eat.

The guidelines were simple enough to obey. They could enjoy everything else in this magnificent garden; only one tree, the one that was in the middle of the garden was forbidden.

The crafty serpent turned God's truth into a question, causing even Eve to wonder. Her fascination led to curiosity. Suddenly, she notices how beautiful the fruit looks and salivates to how delicious it must taste. This fruit was going to make her wise. She was going to become like God. Not only did she eat of the forbidden fruit, but she also shared it with her husband, who was apparently standing right next to her. They both disobeyed God's command and because of this sin, the whole human race has suffered. (Read the full account of this story in Genesis 3.)

A Noble MINDset

As women, we too can fall into a similar trap like Eve. We can allow the enemy to cause us to doubt and be deceived. It takes a noble woman to know how to harness the powerful mind God has given her. Just like I disconnected the call from the so-called IRS, you have to disconnect from what is untrue. When I think of a powerful mind, these descriptive words come to my mind: strong, stable, healthy, positive, wisdom, and capability.

Let's look at some practical ways we can establish a noble "**MIND**set."

Manage your thoughts. 2 Corinthians 10:5

says, "We demolish arguments and every pretension that sets itself up against the knowledge of God, and we take captive every thought to make it obedient to Christ" (NIV). In simple terms, our thoughts need to line up with the thoughts of Christ. We have control over our thoughts. Our thoughts will control our behavior. The right thoughts will produce the right actions and then generate healthy emotions.

Intentional thinking. It is important to know what to think. Philippians 4:8 gives us the guidelines for our thought life. "Finally, brethren, whatever is **true**, whatever is **honorable**, whatever is **right**, whatever is **pure**, whatever is **lovely**, whatever *is of **good*** **repute**, if there is any **excellence** and, if anything **worthy of praise**, let your mind dwell on these things." This should be our daily prayer as we filter through all the "stuff" that goes through our mind on a daily basis. We are commanded here to think about what is true.

Oh friend, how often we focus on what's not true, whether that is about God, others or ourselves. The enemy is constantly feeding us toxic information that is far from the truth. It takes a powerful mind to be intentional about thinking and meditating on what is true.

Nourish the soul. The soul is made up of the mind, will, and emotions. I shared earlier that the word "healthy" is one of the phrases that describes a sharp mind. Just as our body requires beneficial nutrients, our mind also needs healthy nourishment. Romans 12:2 says, "And do not be conformed to this world, but be transformed by the renewing of your mind..." How does one renew her mind? It is a constant process of making it new again and again. Cleaning away the rubbish with the truth.

If you pick up a newspaper or turn on the TV, it won't be long before you are overwhelmed by the current events of this world. Being aware of what is taking place around us is important. However, at the same time, we have to be cautious that we don't get sucked into it.

At times, you just need to take a mental break. Jesus set a perfect example for us. There were times in His ministry here on earth where He just had to pull away. He found that quiet spot to meditate and commune with His Father.

I know it is not easy. Especially as women, we can feel guilty, taking a break from housework, daily routine, and our careers. To stay healthy and mentally sharp, it is imperative. Stress not only affects our mind, but it will also eventually affect our body. Give yourself permission to take a break. Meditate on scripture, journal, or listen to worship music or just do something creative. Sometimes just a nice walk, some sunshine, and fresh air are a welcoming change. Whatever you choose to do, it will change your perspective, refreshing and renewing your mindset.

Deal with negativity. Are you that person who sees the glass as half empty or half full? It's all a matter of perspective. Life will happen. There will be disappointments, unexpected events, and challenges. How we handle these situations will depend greatly on our mental capability and strength.

Having a negative or critical spirit is not an attractive quality. Now, I am not talking about having a bad day or a temporary feeling of gloominess. I am talking about someone who is always negative.

A negative spirit is like a poison that will cause destruction. Negativity and being critical is a sign of unresolved issues. Usually, this stems from a past hurt, unforgiveness, or a poor self-image. An external source has caused an internal "dis-ease." Sadly and yet truthfully, the percentage of the American population that has become dependent on antidepressants is quite alarming. According to a survey done by the Centers Control for Disease in 2008, over 11% of Americans aged 12 years and older take antidepressant medication. Women are more likely to take antidepressants than men. The study also revealed that antidepressants are the third most common drug to be prescribed. An article in *The New York Times*, August 2013, reported that one in 10 Americans take antidepressants. Not only are physicians prescribing these medications, but the patients are also demanding to have them. The disheartening thing about these statistics is that people have become dependent on medication and accepted it as a way of coping with life.

God never designed for us to live life in this manner. He wants us to experience life and life more abundantly (John 10:10). We can't change the events of the past or the causes of pain and "dis-ease," but we can improve our response to these situations. We can choose to forgive, accept healing, and learn to view ourselves in light of God's truth. You have to be willing and open to deal with the heart of the matter, which is the cause of your negativity.

It is a heart issue. The Bible is very clear that there is a mind-heart connection. Proverbs 4:23-24 says, "Above all else, guard your heart, for everything you do flows from it. Keep your mouth free of perversity; keep corrupt talk far from your lips." What is in your heart, your thoughts, feelings, and beliefs will eventually come out of your mouth. It will reveal the condition of your heart.

Dear sister, what comes out of our mouths should be encouraging, life building, and seasoned with grace. We know that it is not about the sticks and stones that might break our bones, but it is the words that are spoken that can break our spirit.

Therefore, we have to be mindful of what we are saying. There are numerous scriptures in the Bible to guide us in polishing up our speech. As a wife and a mom, it is critical that the words you speak to your husband and children are words of life. In James 1:19 we can read these words, "This you know, my beloved brethren. But let everyone be quick to hear, **slow to speak** and slow to anger."

When our two boys were younger, we would have family devotions. One night we wanted to teach them about the power of their words and the effects that it can have on others. We used an object lesson to illustrate this topic. We gathered together a tube of toothpaste and a paper plate. My husband proceeded to squeeze the entire contents of the tube of toothpaste onto the paper plate. Then he asked the boys which one of them would be able to put the toothpaste back into the tube. He offered a monetary prize to the one who could conquer this feat. Of course, the money was enticing, but both boys realized that they could not put the toothpaste back. This teaching allowed us to share with them that what comes out of our mouths cannot be taken back. What we spew out in anger and frustration can cause damage and pain.

So, let's go back to how to deal with negativity. We have identified that it is not healthy and that it can cause damage. Now, how do we manage it? The answer is in the Word of God. First, you have to set your mind on things above. (Read Colossians 3, the entire chapter.) Secondly, choose to respond versus react. Our response should always be from a heart of love. (Philippians 2) The third step is the right emotions will follow. Isaiah 26:3 promises, "You will keep in perfect peace those whose minds are steadfast because they trust in you." Peace is not a gift you can purchase with money, the peace the world gives is temporary, but God's peace is eternal. Who wouldn't want such a precious gift? Let your mindset produce peace in every area of your life.

Character Matters

Your identity determines who you are. Your character reveals your internal "make-up." The character developed by your belief system and values. What I believe about myself and who I am will be exemplified in my words, actions, and behavior.

Perhaps, another way to state this would be to say that your identity reveals *who* you are and your character reveals *what* is inside of you. A genuine nobility of a woman and what sets her apart with a mark of distinction is her excellence of character. Yes, character matters!

The apostle Peter encourages women in 1 Peter 3, to put more emphasis on cultivating the qualities of our inward beauty. This goes against what we see as a cultural norm today. The emphasis is on the outside, the hair, makeup, nails, skin, body shape and the list goes on and on. Please don't mistake me, I am all for looking beautiful, applying a little make-up, and looking presentable. I don't think this is the issue that Peter was addressing. It seems that during that time, just like today, things were out of balance. Women were spending time, and money on outward adornments. They were presenting themselves in a way that was not modest or appropriate. If you are not careful, your outward appearance can depict an image of you that is not true. "And let not your adornment be *merely* external-braiding the hair, and wearing gold jewelry, or putting on dresses; but *let it be* the hidden person of the heart, with the imperishable quality of a gentle and quiet spirit, which is precious in the sight of God" (1 Peter 3:3-4).

The Bible also tells us that God looks at the heart while man looks at the outward appearance. In our humanness, we tend to judge people by what they look like without taking the time to discover what is inside of them. The Bible is full of examples of individuals that God selected for a particular purpose based on what He saw inside of them, not what they looked like on the outside.

Dear friend, your character is critical. It will proceed you, and it will determine your success and destiny in life. Stop and ponder for a moment, and ask yourself this question: What does my character reveal about me?

Three women in history have stood out to me. As a young girl in elementary school, I loved reading the stories of Florence Nightingale, founder of modern nursing, and Clara Barton, founder of the American Red Cross. They were larger than life to me. I was fascinated by their sacrifice and unselfishness to serve wounded soldiers during the war. I secretly wished and dreamed that I could be brave and courageous like them. What stands out to me most about these women is that they never tooted their own horn. They were not trying to make it into all the history books. They were simple and quietly served their purpose.

Another lady that has been a role model for me is Mother Teresa. What an amazing woman. She might have been small in size and frame, but the impact she has made is enormous. She made it her mission and passion to love the rejected. She founded orphanages for children who were on the streets of Calcutta. I was baffled when I discovered that she was not a native of India. She never married nor had her own biological children, yet she became a mother to thousands of children, and she was fondly called, *Mother Teresa.* In her words, she said, "Of all the rights of a woman, the greatest is to be a mother." What caused her to give up all that she could have acquired? It goes back to purpose. She was burdened by what she saw, and she was determined to do something.

These women and countless others in history books and the Bible are examples for us of the character being molded and displayed. Ruth was defined as a woman of noble character, Abigail for being a peacemaker, the Proverbs 31 woman for her wisdom, and Hannah for her graciousness and patience. These women took their life challenges and allowed it to build their character. As John Maxwell so eloquently writes in his book, *The 21 Indispensable Qualities of a Leader*, "Crisis doesn't necessarily make character, but it certainly does reveal it. Adversity is a crossroads that makes a person choose one of two paths: character or compromise." I invite you, dear friend, to choose the path of character.

Character Building

Here are some guidelines for character building:

1. **Decide to make the right decisions.** Choose to think the right thoughts about God, yourself and others. Your thinking controls your actions and reactions. Thoughts are like seeds; you will grow what you plant. Proverbs 23:7 says, "For as he thinks within himself, so he is."
2. **Be a fruit bearer.** Choose to display the fruit of the spirit in your walk and talk. Learn how to respond to others and life circumstances. Reactions are explosions that cause damage. Galatians 5:22-23 says, "But the fruit of the Spirit is love, joy, peace, patience, kindness, goodness, faithfulness, gentleness, self-control; against such things there is no law."
3. **Adorn yourself with meekness and quietness.** Meekness is not weakness, but rather a quality of strength that is under (self) control. There is a time for everything, a time to speak and a time to be

silent. It is not necessary to always share a piece of your mind. Someone cleverly noted that listen and silent have the same six letters. Learn to listen and think before you speak. Words are powerful, "Death and life are in the power of the tongue, and those who love it will eat its fruit" (Proverbs 18:21).

As noble women, God has given us the power of influence. Our very words, behavior, and actions are powerful enough to change our husbands, children, family, and coworkers and those around us. Let us be intentional in choosing our words so that they are life builders. Let us make sure that the things we do are honorable, and that our actions show the pure motives and intentions of our hearts. Proverbs 14:1 says, "The wise woman builds her house, but the foolish tears it down with her own hands."

My challenge to you: choose today to be a lady that is wise and one who desires to build a home that is nurturing, stable and peaceful. Your words and behavior can be detrimental, and destructive to your family. Model to your children what you want them to become.

"Kind words can be short and easy to speak, but their echoes are truly endless."

~Mother Teresa

- Live your life by principles.
- Be disciplined.
- Have discernment.
- Walk in dignity.
- Establish a noble MINDset.

PROCLAMATIONS

- I will live my life by principles.
- I can manage my life by creating order.
- I am clothed with strength and dignity.
- I will guard my mind and mouth.
- My character matters.

Personal Reflection

1. What are the three principles discussed at the beginning of this chapter? Jot down some thoughts about each principle.

2. How can you establish a noble MINDset? Which practical guideline do you need to implement?

3. Do you have someone who has been a role model? What stands out to you about their character? (If you can, write a thank-you note to them.)

4. God has given man the power of authority. What did He give the woman? The power of______________________________. How can you use this power?

Pillar IV - Productivity

"Time management is life management." Robin Sharma

Time Management

As a young wife and mother, I often felt overwhelmed with all the daily routines of keeping house. I considered myself to be an organized and a rather meticulous person. My childhood upbringing and living in a dormitory through most of my schooling years had taught me responsibility and discipline. But, I had this feeling that there were not enough hours in my day to accomplish all that I needed to get done. I was aware of what needed to be done. I lacked the skills to create a plan to make it all work.

It's easy to manage one person, but to administer a household of four, at the time, two adults and two kids, was entirely different, and that's where my struggle began. I just didn't know how to prioritize my time and develop a plan that I could follow. I found myself spinning circles but not accomplishing much. As a child, I just followed the rules and did what I was told and *voilà* it worked out. But here I was, with no manual or guidance on how to run a home or take care of a family.

I was determined to be a perfect wife and mother, so I set out on my quest to find the solution to my problem. This was before, Pinterest, Google, and all the wonderful things we have at our fingertips today to help us navigate through life. I was at the Christian bookstore one day, and there on the shelf, I saw the book that changed my life. The book was appropriately titled, *More Hours in My Day* by Emilie Barnes. I took Emilie Barnes home with me that day and devoured her book. I learned how to organize myself, my home, and children and how to save money and run my home like a business. I made a schedule, meal plans, shopping lists, and found that I did have enough hours in a day. I just needed to learn to plan and manage my time. The old familiar saying is true: *"People don't plan to fail, they fail to plan."*

Planning is key to productivity.

Planning is key to productivity. You see without a plan, I was just spinning around in circles, and I did not see the results of my accomplishments. Therefore, I felt frustrated, like stringing pearls on a chain without a knot at the end. But once I learned that I could plan my day and chart out my course for the week, I could see the results of my labor of love.

At our church, we encourage people to use the word productive instead of busy. We use statements like, "I am productive, or I have/had a productive week." There is a big difference in being productive versus busy. Busy can mean that you are actively doing things, but they are meaningless. Let me explain, before I discovered the book by Emilie Barnes, I was doing things but not accomplishing much. I tried to do the laundry, clean the bedrooms, and clean the refrigerator, and had great intentions to finish these tasks, but because my time management skills were not perfected, I only completed half of each of these tasks. So at the end of the day, I felt like I had not fulfilled what I had intended to accomplish.

When I realized I could be productive with a little planning and time management, I was on board. I learned to assign tasks for different days of the week, and I also learned that setting a beginning and ending time kept me motivated to complete my tasks. These principles helped me as a homeschool mom to organize our school days. Now, did every day work like clock-work? Certainly not. There were interruptions and unexpected events that came up. Interestingly enough, even though our schedule shifted during those times, it gave me the freedom to restructure our lives.

Another habit I formed that helped me to stay organized and on course was to write everything down. I am a bit old school when it comes to calendars and day timers. I know there are many digital tools available, and if you are one of those techy kinds of people, go for it. For me what has worked and continued to work is to keep a day timer where I record all the appointments and events. I update it weekly or as needed. It is my map; so at a glance, I know what each day, week, and month will look like. I also have a wall calendar so the family can get a view of what is happening day to day and month to month. My lifesaving tool is a spiral steno notebook. I am a list maker, and this is where I keep an ongoing list of everything I need to do from sending out bills to grocery lists. I find it rewarding to check things off and see my accomplishments. This steno notebook travels everywhere with me, yes, even on vacation. Because I like structure and order, I still make lists on vacations.

I also like planning ahead. Get the laundry sorted the night before, set out breakfast items, and prepare lunches in advance. These little steps of preparation can be beneficial in the long run. Careful planning and preparation are essential components for success. Maybe you are a spontaneous person who likes to go with the flow. It might be hard and feel unnatural to follow a schedule or plan. I encourage you to try. It will probably require some discipline, but remember with God's help; anything is possible. You will enjoy the freedom it will bring and the amount of stress that will be reduced.

In her book, Emilie Barnes notes that "eighty-five percent of our stress is caused by disorganization. The benefits of order in our lives are significant: Stress is relieved, hours redeemed, and joy regained." The moment I read this sentence years ago, it dawned on me that I could do something about that eighty-five percent of stress.

I took the challenge and became a manager of my home. Things came into order, and a system was established. As a noble woman, we are the heart of our homes. We set the tone and the atmosphere that transforms a house into a home. Our families cannot function in chaos and disorder. Be a role model for your family and teach them how to live a life of order.

It blesses my heart when my husband comes home and can see and feel that order is in the home. He has often commented on how welcoming it is for him enter and enjoy a peaceful atmosphere from a long day of work. He doesn't have to step over the laundry to get into the house, or find the bedroom in a state of chaos. The kitchen sink is not piled up with dirty dishes from the week. The couches are not covered up with clean clothes and towels that need folding. This not a picture of a noble woman's home. Before you close the book and give up, let me share with you that we do live in our home. You will see some dust, a dish or two in the sink or a basket of laundry, however, my point is that there is still order and structure in place. These things are manageable and will be handled. When you let things go for too long, you will become overwhelmed and decide to live in your disorder. Your mess will cause stress!

I encourage you to become a modern day Proverbs 31 productive woman. As I stated earlier, productivity will produce results; busyness doesn't. When you are productive, you won't have time to be negative, critical, and complaining. Rather, you will appreciate that your work has a purpose, and your attitude will be one that is positive. You will understand the value of your time and other people's time.

Excellence vs. Perfection

I made a statement earlier in this chapter that I was determined to become a "perfect" wife and mother. And wow, did I strive to be perfect. I've always had a perfectionistic tendency. Without fully realizing it, I wanted everything I did to reflect my perfect touch. In a way, I suppose I was expecting others to applaud my perfectionism.

Looking back on those years of attempting to be perfect, I can acknowledge that I was racing the clock against myself. I had set the bar so high for myself, and I worked hard, perhaps too hard to reach that standard. In my eyes everything had to be done right; there was tiny room for error. I set the standard high for my husband and children, too. And when they didn't measure up to my standard, I became frustrated and angry. I felt their imperfections were a reflection on me. I couldn't see at the time what I was doing to myself or my family.

Then one summer, my deliverance came. A dear lady was invited to speak at the church we were attending at the time. One night she taught on the difference between excellence and perfection. My life turned the corner; I could almost hear the chains of bondage fall off me, and I embraced liberty. I realized I did not have to try to be perfect. I never could attain that goal. I learned through her teaching that God wants us to pursue excellence. What a revelation that was to me. I had never known that these two words, although often used interchangeably, really had different meanings.

The definitions of these words from the dictionary don't explain fully how these words differ. But, I want you to grasp the meaning, so you, too, dear friend, can be set free from trying to be perfect.

So let's look at perfectionism. It is an attitude, a belief that everything must be perfect. There are no gray areas; it's black or white. The motivation of perfectionism is fear, the fear of failure. It is also pressure driven with unrealistic expectations. This mindset will lead to anger, frustration, and control. Perfectionistic people lack self-worth and doubt themselves. They can be judgmental, critical, discounting their successes and focusing on their failures. Perfectionism concentrates on the outcome.

Now let's take a look at excellence. The attitude

of excellence is a willingness to learn from mistakes and be taught. The motivation of excellence is faith, trusting God with the results after doing your ultimate best. Excellence is being confident and having a healthy self-esteem. It also achieves patience and balance. Excellence focuses on the process and the journey, rather than the destination.

I hope that you can see the marked difference between these two words. As you ponder these descriptions, consider how you want to be defined. A perfectionistic person seeks the approval of man. A noble woman of excellence will obtain the approval of God.

"Whatever you do, do your work heartily, as for the Lord rather than for men; knowing that from the Lord you will receive the reward of the inheritance.
It is the Lord Christ whom you serve"
(Colossians 3:23-24).

It is Good!

We've learned a lot in this chapter, the importance of time management and how to pursue excellence. I want to share one more thought that fits in with what we have been discussing.

Be content with what you have done. Do whatever you need to do in excellence and then just check it off your list as DONE! This system also goes for things others may do for you, too.

My husband taught me a long time ago that it is important to be objective instead of subjective. When he is home in the evening, he likes to serve me by washing the dishes. It is a very thoughtful and loving gesture.

I made the mistake when I was that "perfectionistic" person to criticize the way he washed the dishes. In my eyes, he did not do them right because they were not done the way I would do them. I can laugh about it now, but we did have some serious dishwashing conversations. My dear husband had to point out to me that I needed to be grateful they were done and not be so subjective of how they were washed. Thankfully, he still washes dishes on occasion today, and I just smile and thank him. It is not a big deal. The fact of the matter is that it is done, and that is good enough.

God could have created the world in a nanosecond. The Bible tells us how He created the earth in six days and spoke things into existence. As you read about the creation in Genesis 1, you will notice this phrase: "And God saw that it was good."

You can only do what you can do and then you just have to say: "It is good." Remember, it's not about perfection, but excellence. That means that the more you practice doing whatever it is you are doing, it will become better and better. Be sure to set realistic goals. You can't climb Mt. Everest without planning, preparing, and setting goals. Climb hills first, and then you can reach mountains.

For the past few years, I have taught a fifth-grade writing class. During the first class, I ask the students to write a few paragraphs about their summer. This is an in-class assignment, which they hand to me. I hold on to these papers, and at the end of nine months for our very last class, I staple their first assignment as well as their last assignment together and hand it back to them. It is fun to see their expressions. Some of them can't believe how poorly they used to write. They are truly amazed at their vocabulary and sentence structure. Their parents are also thrilled to see the improvement. It is also rewarding to me as a teacher to see the progress. And this is what it is all about: progression to attain excellence.

"For I am confident of this very thing, that He who began a good work in you will perfect it until the day of Christ Jesus" (Philippians 1:6).

Points to Ponder

- Planning is key to productivity.
- Learn to manage time.
- Become a planner.
- Disorganization spells-STRESS!
- Learn to live a life of order.
- Pursue excellence not perfection.

Proclamations

- I will be productive.
- I will bring order into my life.
- I will pursue excellence.
- I will learn to say, "It is good!"

Personal Reflection

1. Do you struggle with time management? If so, then you need to record where and how you are spending your time. This will help you to identify what your time "eaters" are.

2. Change your thought process from being busy to becoming productive. Now create a plan. Start out small, perhaps just a weekly menu or grocery list. Be consistent and then add something else you would like to tackle.

3. Ecclesiastes 3:1 says, "There is an appointed time for everything. And there is a time for every event under heaven-" Do you have a hobby, a class you want to take or a book you want to read? Create time in your schedule to do things you enjoy doing.

4. In your words, write down the definitions of *perfection* and *excellence. Remember the goal is excellence.*

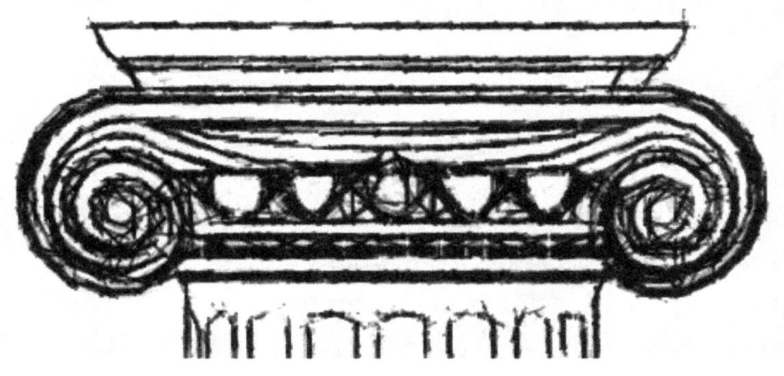

Pillar V - People and Projects

"There is an appointed time for everything. And there is a time for every event under heaven"
Ecclesiastes 3:1

I do not claim to be a mechanic, nor do I know a whole lot about cars. But over the years of driving, I have learned to pay attention to various indicators. When the oil light comes on, it's time for an oil change. When I hear the brakes grinding, it's time for new brake pads. Ignoring these signals can cause damage to the car and cost a pretty penny.

Not too long ago, I kept noticing that every time I drove up the hill entering our subdivision, the car seemed to pull to the right. We took the car to our local mechanic. He informed us that the tread on the tires was pretty low, and the pulling to one side was due to improper balance and alignment.

We replaced all four tires, balanced and aligned the wheels. The mechanic also placed a sticker, on my window, to remind me that I needed to return for a balance checkup after driving only a few hundred miles. Since then another sticker was placed telling me to go back after a few thousand miles of driving to check the balance of the tires.

Priorities

"Most of us spend too much time on what is urgent and not enough time on what is important."
Stephen R. Covey

You know life is like this, too. You have to have things in balance to be able to function properly. When things get out of balance, you will sense it in one area or another, a pulling in one direction or another. You will find that some areas of your life are ignored.

We live in a world that is fast paced that demands our time and energy. We have children to care for, household responsibilities, financial pressures, and deadlines to meet. So how does one manage life, so it doesn't manage us?

It boils down to priorities. You have to distinguish between what's important and what's urgent. You cannot become an emergency vehicle for everybody's problems. You will find yourself running around town putting out fires. You were not created to manage other people's lives.

Years ago, God gave me the revelation that I was

to be *caring* towards people, not *carrying* people. My gifting and calling is to serve people and help them. I enjoy it, but I also have to manage it. It is easy to cross the line from helping to enabling.

Take time to evaluate and find out what your priorities are. Where are you spending the most time? What do you enjoy doing? Are you productive? We talked about this before, and I simply cannot stress the importance of developing a plan. Utilizing a system will help you to be productive. I have created an acronym for the word **PLAN**.

Priorities—What are they? Make a list.

Learn to use a calendar. It will help you to manage your time.

Allow time for yourself. Take time for yourself. You are important.

No is not a dirty word. It is okay to say, "No" without feeling guilty. Know your limits.

Relationships

I am so thankful for the people God has placed in my life. I have found comfort, strength, and encouragement in these relationships. We were not created to live alone or to go through life alone. God created us to be interdependent because we need each other.

Medical research has also proven that those who have strong relationships live longer, are healthier, feel happier and can deal with stress and also feel richer. Just increasing friendships made people feel like they had a 50% increase in their income.

So there's no denying that people are valuable to our well-being, and we need people. We need to make people a priority in our lives. In our fast-paced, busy world it is easy to neglect spending time and to invest in the lives of individuals. We make excuses that we lack time. We may have the best intentions, but we don't add actions to our intentions.

It is important to realize that regardless of what

you may have going on in your life, people always come before projects. Projects can wait. There have been several times that I have had to drop what I was doing to pray with someone, provide a meal or just sit with someone. Sure, it might have disrupted my schedule momentarily, but the rewards of being a channel for God to use has far outweighed the interruption.

A scripture that comes to mind is Proverbs 11:25, "The generous man will be prosperous, and he who waters will himself be watered." We should seek to be generous in sowing seeds of kindness, love, and compassion. It is nourishing to focus on the needs of others.

We must put first things first, which means we have to **prioritize our relationships.**

1. God must be our number one priority. It is not enough to be a believer in word only; you must cultivate a relationship with God. Just as you would communicate with a friend, God desires to commune with you. Set apart time each day to pray and read His Word. His Word is a love letter to you. Allot time to listen to Him and write down what He tells you.

2. "But a woman who fears the Lord, she shall be praised" (Proverbs 31:30).

3. Spend time with your husband. After God had

created man, He realized Adam needed a helpmate, a companion. He created Eve, not from the dust of the earth, but from a rib that He took from Adam. She would be that missing element in his life. She would complete and complement him.

4. Wives, it is important for you to respect your husbands. It is a command from God, and it is beautifully written in Ephesians 5:33. The Amplified Bible says it this way, "Let the wife see that she respects and reverences her husband—that she notices him, regards him, honors him, prefers him, venerates and esteems him; and that she defers to him, praises him and loves and admires him exceedingly." Wow! Stormie Omartian, the author of *The Power of a Praying Wife,* simplifies it with three "P's": pray, praise, and pamper. And I have added my explanations in parenthesis: pray for him (not about him), praise (admire him verbally), and pamper (shower him with kind and loving acts).

5. I've had the opportunity to speak to wives as a group when my husband and I have conducted marriage seminars. Inevitably, there are a few women that have sought me out and shared that they cannot possibly respect their husbands because of certain behaviors they have displayed. Does that mean they are exempt from

respecting their husbands? No, it doesn't; this is a command that God has given us as wives. I encourage these ladies to still show respect for the place of authority that God has given to the man as the head of the household and the head of her. This is not condoning his behavior, but rather walking in obedience to God and trusting God to be in charge of the changes that need to occur. It is a tough road to walk, and my heart always aches for these wives. We have to trust God and allow Him to do His perfect work in the lives of our husbands. We cannot do our job and God's job.

6. Prayer is vital and crucial. My husband and I have been married for almost 26 years. Our relationship was birthed in prayer, and we have prayed together virtually every single day. When distance separates us, we pray together over the phone. Prayer is communication with God with our hearts united. It is the glue that strengthens and keeps our relationship intact. Not only is it important to have an individual prayer life, but as a couple to come before the throne of God as a united front. It's hard to be in discord when you know you have to come before God. Over the years, we have kept "Faith Journals," noting down our prayer requests and the answers God has given us.

7. We also pray with our children on a regular basis. When they were younger, we planned family devotion time. I am thankful for the seeds of faith we planted in their lives. As they have gotten older, we have remained close. Prayer and our faith in God continue to keep us united.

8. Spend time with family and this includes children. They need to know that they are valued. Spend time with them. Consider spending quality time instead of quantity of time. Create memories that will last for years to come. Capture these moments with pictures. Celebrate birthdays and life events together. If you have young children, plan activities that are age appropriate and engaging. When our boys were very young, my husband took them on father-son retreats. He designed t-shirts for them to wear and planned out a weekend of activities. He also spent time praying for them and giving them a blessing. You don't have to spend a lot of money. Some of our best memories are the little things we did at home. A movie night with popcorn or a midnight trip to pick up some ice cream one hot summer. These are simple things to do, and they have lasting effects.

9. My parents live in India, yet with modern technology, we can remain close and connected. I am also close with my siblings and their families

who live in different states. We have been intentional in keeping in touch and celebrating holidays together.

10. Friends and friendships come in different levels. There will be those few very close friends that are part of your inner circle. Take time to fellowship and communicate with them. These are the people who will keep you accountable, pray with you, and for you and will show up just to be with you. We live in an age where technology makes it so much easier to stay in touch. Take advantage of Skype, Facebook, and various other means to stay connected. As much as I love writing letters, those days are gone. We live in the e-world, so e-mail and e-card your friends.

11. Co-workers and acquaintances, they also need to know you care. You may not be able to invest a lot of time in them. But as a noble woman and a believer, you can make an impact in their lives. You may not be able to participate in all the things they invite you to, but you can still make them a part of your life. Look for opportunities to show them God's love without being "preachy."

12. For those of you who may find yourself in a season of singleness, it is so important that you cultivate healthy relationships. Being planted in the right church allows you to have a family. We

tell our single ladies and single moms that the church is their "covering," and we do include them in our activities and make sure they feel welcome and are a part of the community of believers. We reach out to their children by spending time with them and loving them. They need to experience healthy, safe relationships.

Positioned to Influence

We just discussed the variety of people in our lives and how important it is to spend time with them. When God created man, he gave him the *power of authority*. When He created the woman, He bestowed upon her the *power of influence.*

Dear friend, you were designed to be a noble lady. God took time to build and fashion you, and in doing so He fashioned you with **three qualities**:

1. Virtue—in her book, *Beautiful in God's Eyes,* Elizabeth George shares some powerful insights on this word virtue. This term was typically used to describe an army in the Old Testament. We see that it is also used to describe the Proverbs 31 woman, as a woman of virtue. She is an army within herself. She is capable of mental toughness and physical energy which are traits of an army. This Hebrew word refers to a *force* and is used to mean *able, capable, mighty, strong, valiant, powerful, efficient, wealthy, and worthy.* What a beautiful description of who you are, dear noble

woman. You are fully equipped; it's up to you to see what God has placed inside of you.

2. Influence—According to the dictionary, this word means having the capacity or power to produce effects on the actions, behavior, and opinions of others. As I mentioned earlier, God has bestowed upon the woman the power of influence. A wise, noble woman will choose to use that power to elevate the lives of others. She will be careful to make the right choices with her words, actions and behavior. As we mentioned to earlier in Proverbs 14:1, "The wise woman builds her house, but the foolish tears it down with her own hands." It saddens me to think that some women have abused the power that God has given them and have caused destruction to their homes.

3. A great Biblical example of a woman who used her power of influence is Esther. We looked at her life earlier, and we could see that she used that power to gain the king's favor to save her people. The Proverbs 31 woman also used her influence in such a way that her husband became well known. She believed in her man, and she encouraged him to pursue his potential. She willingly and diligently took care of her household, and she gave her husband as a gift to society. He was able to flourish in his purpose and calling because of her influence. He did not

have to be concerned about his household or his children; his noble, virtuous wife took care of them. What an example for each of us to follow.

4. Peter also encourages women to be submissive to their unbelieving husbands, because their spouses may be won by the power of influence without a word. Sometimes, it is better to be silent and let our actions of love, kindness, and goodness speak. "In the same way, you wives, be submissive to your own husbands so that even if any of them are disobedient to the word, they may be won without a word by the behavior of their wives" (I Peter 3:1).

5. Beauty—God created women to be beautiful. He fashioned women with curves, soft skin, and lovely hair. These characteristics can make a woman look attractive and beautiful. Authentic beauty, however, begins on the inside and becomes an outward manifestation. "Your adornment must not be merely external-braiding the hair, and wearing gold jewelry, or putting on dressed; but let it be the hidden person of the heart, with the imperishable quality of a gentle and quiet spirit, which is precious in the sight of God" (I Peter 3:3-4).

6. I charge you, dear friend, to take your rightful place as a noble woman full of virtue, beauty, and influence.

- Distinguish between what is important versus what is urgent.
- Determine your priorities.
- People always come before projects.
- Women have the power of influence.

PROCLAMATIONS

- I will focus on what is important.
- I will determine my priorities.
- I will make time for people.
- I will make time for myself.
- I will cultivate healthy relationships.
- I am a woman of influence.

Personal Reflection

1. Take time to reflect and write down your priorities.

2. Are you spending time on what is urgent or what is important? What changes do you need to make?

3. Read Proverbs 31:30. Do a word study on the word "fears."

4. Review the acronym for PLAN. Complete this phrase. *"If I had time I would……"*

5. Create a list of things you enjoy doing. Make the time to do something for yourself. You are worth it.

Pillar VI - Pursue Health

"Health is a state of body. Wellness is a state of being." J.Stanford

There's a lot of buzz about health these days. Walk into a bookstore and you will see a variety of books that will tell you what to eat, what not to eat, how to eat it, and when to eat. It can get overwhelming, and the information overload can confuse and frustrate, to say the least.

I have been guilty of purchasing the latest and greatest books on health and weight loss. They promised me weight loss if I followed their plan. Sure, I was sold and I would set out to follow the plan, and then lo and behold after not seeing results, I would give up. This has been a cycle for me. I'm not saying these books and their diet plans don't work. People do get results. But it is important to note that everyone's body is different, and there are many factors to consider. What works for one person may not necessarily work for another.

Women struggle with their weight and appearance more than men. Magazines, TV shows, celebrities and other iconic personalities are always featured with their trim waistlines and sleek physiques. Who wouldn't want to look flawless and try to resemble those we see in the public eye? (Just know that their pictures are photoshopped to achieve beauty and perfection.)

The diet and weight loss industry have tapped into a money making business. They tell you just enough to hook you and sell you just a limited amount of information or product to make you a repeat customer. Their plan works as long as you are using their products. The moment you get off the plan, the weight comes back, and the struggle begins again. I guess that's why they call it yo-yo dieting.

> Our awesome Creator provided everything we need to sustain and heal us.

The very word "dieting" does something to our brains. It causes us to believe we have to eliminate our favorite foods. We can't have this, and we can't have that. Just think as soon as you hear the word "can't," something inside of you desires to partake in what you "can't" have. You feel like you are missing out, losing something.

Think of Eve in the Garden of Eden. As soon as the serpent said, "Did God say you **can't** eat of any tree in the garden?" (paraphrase mine) That trick question caused her to eat that which was forbidden. And the rest is history, as they say.

I am thankful for the new revelation and all that we are learning today about health, diet, and nutrition. Health is a fascinating field to me, and I enjoy reading and learning about how to care for our bodies and our health. Knowledge is power and educating yourself in this area is important. The more I learn and grasp information, I am awestruck at how fearfully and wonderfully we were created. Our awesome Creator provided everything we need to sustain and heal us.

Taking Care of Your Body

Journey with me as we discuss the aspect of caring for our temple, which is our body. We are made up of spirit, soul, and body. Up to this point, we have talked about our spiritual makeup and the realm of the soul, which encompasses the mind, will, and emotions. The body is also equally important as it makes up the third realm of who we are.

Romans 12:1 says, "I urge you, therefore, brethren, by the mercies of God, to present your bodies a living and holy sacrifice, acceptable to God, which is your spiritual service of worship." One of the words in the dictionary that defines what sacrifice means is "surrendered", which is giving up something in exchange for something that is better.

As I read this verse, it seems to be telling me that I must be willing to surrender my body to God to please Him. In other words, completely give up myself to God.

When we present something to God, we want to give Him our ultimate best. In the Old Testament, when a sacrifice was made, it was usually some small animal that was without blemish. When we surrender our bodies to God, it is an act of worship. I am not free to do whatever I want to do because my body belongs to God.

Not only does my body belong to God, but it also houses Him. My body is a temple where God abides. His residence is in me. I can't take Him to places that dishonor Him; I can't feed Him what is unhealthy, and I can't wear what does not mirror His character.

Dear noble woman, do not take your body lightly. It may only be an earthly suit to house your spirit man, but it belongs to God, and you are ultimately responsible for how you take care of it. Suppose you borrowed an elegant gown from your friend for a gala. How would you take care of that expensive dress? You're right the whole night you would be extra careful not to spill anything or let any damage come to it.

Let me share these words with you, "Do you not know that you are a temple of God and that the Spirit of God dwells in you?" (1 Corinthians 3:16). So, let us learn together how we can take care of our temple. These are just **basic principles and truths** for each one of us to follow.

1. Your body needs nourishment. Feed your body what it needs not what it wants. Educate yourself, read labels, and make wise choices. Stay away from the "white" stuff, packaged foods and those items containing chemicals and preservatives. A good rule is to eat what God created. Limit your intake of sweets. Notice I did not say eliminate, just limit. Eat until you are satisfied, not full. Plan ahead and carry healthy snacks with you. At the restaurant go for the lighter options. Savor your food and you will eat less.

2. Drink plenty of water. Your body needs replenishing of fluids. Slicing lemons or berries and adding them to your water is not only refreshing but adds flavor. Stay away from drinks filled with sugar and other unpronounceable chemicals; they don't belong in your body. I enjoy hot beverages, too, and green tea is an excellent choice. If you must sweeten it, add some honey. Hot water with lemons or lemon juice makes a nice detoxifying drink. Coffee in moderation is okay, just don't overload on the flavored creamers and sugar.

3. Sleep and rest are also required. The body needs time to repair itself, and that takes place at night or when you are sleeping for a lengthy period.

Creating a healthy habit of unplugging from electronics at least thirty minutes before going to sleep gives your mind time to come to a state of relaxation. Try to go to bed at the same time each night and wake up in the morning at the same time. You will feel more refreshed with this consistency. My wise husband says that our bodies need sleep, and our minds need rest.

4. You have to move it, move it! Move your body with exercise. Do something you enjoy doing, walking, jogging or working out at a gym. Start slow and set attainable goals. Find a friend to join you and stay accountable to each other. Consistency is the key to success. Small steps will lead to rewards. And that goes for anything in life. Exercise will give you energy, youthfulness, and physical strength. Remember, you are an army within, and you have to stay in shape.

5. Listen to your body. Stay current with your routine doctor visits. Since our diet lacks vitamins and minerals, be sure to supplement with quality vitamins. Practice good hygiene and take care of your body. Read labels, certain cosmetics, lotions, and perfumes contain chemicals that are potentially harmful. Several companies make healthier products for your skin. Do your research and be an educated noble woman.

Well-being vs. Weight Loss

Just a word of caution and wisdom. As women, we can get caught up in numbers, and I am referring to numbers on the scale and size. Now, there are times when numbers regarding your health are critical, and you must pay attention to these numbers. For example blood pressure, blood sugar, and waist measurement and blood count. What the scale tells you should not be ignored if you need to lose some weight. However, don't let numbers define you.

Change your attitude about weight loss to pursue well-being. Focus on being healthy rather than being a particular size. The size will come in time, but you also have to be content to embrace and love yourself in your skin. A healthy self-image will promote a healthy lifestyle. You won't find yourself compromising, but you will learn the art of discipline and self-control. These are beautiful qualities for a noble woman to possess.

The pursuit of well-being focuses on what you will gain. The gaining factor will outweigh the losses or the feeling of being deprived. Think about increasing healthy habits, lifestyle, attitude and enjoying nutritious foods. Your desire to eat the "junk" will diminish, and an occasional treat will be sufficient. Your tastes will change, and you will have the willpower to pass up the cheesecake.

When you focus on the weight loss, you are looking at the numbers on the scale and the dress size. You get depressed thinking of all the sweets you are unwillingly giving up. Then when the temptation arises, you will give in, and it will seem like defeat. You may lose your motivation to start all over again, and then the depression of feeling overweight and fat will take control. Don't set yourself up for failure. Change your outlook and realize it is far healthier to pursue well-being.

It is not going to be easy, and there may be some slips, but keep your eye on the long-term goal. Create a plan and stay committed to it. You will see results, and they will be long lasting. Know that it is God's will for you to prosper in your health. "Beloved, I pray that in all respects you may prosper and be in good health, just as your soul prospers" (3 John 1:2).

Strength and Dignity

I wanted to add this advice in this section about your body. How a woman dresses her body and carries herself reveals her heart and character. I shared this statement with a group of young ladies several years ago: "Dress to look attractive, don't dress to attract" (*Sylvia Banks*).

In essence, what I was sharing with them is that when a woman dresses inappropriately and lacks modesty, she is bound to attract the wrong kind of company. She is sending out a message either knowingly or unknowingly. You see, "Modesty isn't about hiding your body. It's about revealing your dignity" (*Jessica Rey*). I couldn't have said it better; this truly captures the truth of how we should dress.

My two sons are young men in their early twenties. They attend college and work; I was concerned as to how the dress or lack of dress young women clothe themselves with would affect them. We've had some conversations, and they have expressed how unimpressive and what a turn off it is to see a poorly clad lady.

I like what Jenny Williams has to say on this subject: "When a girl or woman dresses immodestly she has no idea the battle a man goes through to focus mentally or keep his thoughts pure. It's a minefield that he is trying to overcome. Ladies, don't be the battle for him to have to fight. Dress in honor for others and God."

> Dress to look attractive, don't dress to attract.

The Proverbs 31 noble woman sets an example for us that we should also follow. She spun her clothes from fine linen, and she chose to wear purple. She didn't skimp; she preferred to be fashionable and classy. Her color of choice, purple, is the color of royalty. She was confident in who she was; she knew her identity and her purpose. She was not concerned about making an impression; she was focused on making an impact.

Please don't mistake me, I love fashion, clothing, jewelry, and all the accessories. I do believe God created us to enjoy these things; the problem arises when we go to the extreme. When you shop, look for pieces that are classy, well made, and items that will not go out of style. Build a wardrobe that will last. There are many ways to buy well-designed clothing for a fraction of the cost. In all honesty, less is more. Owning a few staples pieces of clothing and mixing and matching and accessorizing can go a long way. Fashions will come and go, and you can incorporate the latest style or color to your existing basic wardrobe.

In dressing your body, it is helpful to know your body type. There are five basic body types: hourglass, apple, pear, triangle, and rectangle. Different styles complement certain body types. There are various resources online that can guide you in discovering what is going to flatter your body. I have found this knowledge very helpful in my shopping experiences. I can avoid frustration and maximize my time by looking for pieces that will work for me. Just one more piece of advice, dress age appropriately. It is not becoming to see a middle-aged woman in an outfit created for a teenage body. No, no, this is not what a noble woman looks like who bears the image of God.

Be distinct in your heart, motives, and in the way your dress. "Likewise, I want women to adorn themselves with proper clothing, modestly and discreetly, not with braided hair and gold or pearls or costly garments; but rather by means of good works, as befits women making a claim to godliness" (1 Timothy 2:9-10).

Points to Ponder

- Pursue health and a healthy lifestyle.
- Take care of your temple.
- Focus on well-being over weight loss.
- Practice self-control and self-discipline.
- Don't be defined by numbers.
- "Dress to look attractive, don't dress to attract."

Proclamations

- I will pursue health and be healthy.
- I will take care of my body.
- I will practice self-control and self-discipline.
- I won't let numbers define me.
- I will clothe myself with strength and dignity.

Personal Reflection

1. Read 3 John 1:2. What is this verse saying to you? What can you do to be in good health?

2. What have been your personal struggles with food or weight loss?

3. Establishing healthy habits is key to good health. Write down some habits you would like to incorporate into your lifestyle.

4. Ask yourself, does my way of dressing reflect who I am? Am I following guidelines that honor God?

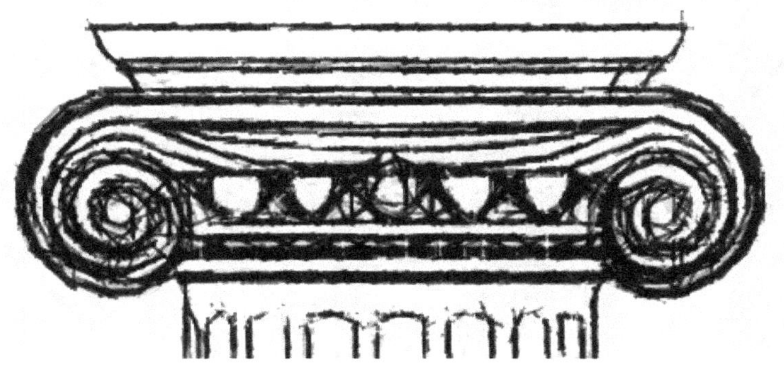

Pillar VII - Profession

"We relish news of heroes, forgetting that we are extraordinary to somebody too." Helen Hayes

When my husband and I agreed that I should be a stay-at-home mom, we realized there would be many sacrifices to make. We may not have the luxuries of life, drive fancy cars, or own a mansion, and we were okay with that. We committed ourselves to our calling, and our focus was not material gain.

I must admit there were times when I felt we were poorer than church mice. We weren't; God provided for all our needs. But you know, you look around and begin to compare what you have to what others have. I took the lyrics of Donna Summer's song, *"She works hard for her money,"* and created my own version to her song, *"She works hard for **no** money!"* Wow, how depressing. But somewhere along the way, my attitude changed.

Your Position

"Bloom where you are planted."

God had to give me a heart transplant not just an attitude adjustment. You see I was happy to be at home and care for our children and eventually homeschool them, but I did not know that what I was doing was my profession. When you have a profession, you receive a nice fat paycheck, right?!

Somewhere in those formative years of being a homemaker, I picked up a book written by Steven and Teri Maxwell. The title gripped me, and suddenly, I realized that my position as a stay-at-home mom was valuable. It was not about the income or lack of it, but rather the outcome and what the results of being a homemaker were going to provide for our family. The title of their book, *Managers of Their Homes,* changed my perspective.

I did not consider myself as a homemaker any longer; I chose to be a domestic engineer. Running and operating my home became like a business to me. I had a mission, and with the help of my supportive husband, we created a vision for our home. We named our homeschool, The Banks Academy of Excellence. Now some 17 years later, we have successfully graduated two sons. Benjamin just graduated from college, and Caleb is still pursuing his degree, and our youngest, Maiya, will begin high school in the fall.

I see the "paycheck" now, and it far greater than anything money could have purchased. Our kids have morals, standards, and a godly lifestyle that they have chosen. Our home is a place of quietness and peace. We enjoy spending time together as a family. In this day and age, many families do not have these benefits and blessings.

For me, my position was in the home, and that's where God wanted me to make my impact. It may be different for you. I will be the first one to tell you that homeschooling is not for everyone. Perhaps you are a full-time mom who juggles a full-time career. Maybe you are single lady attending school and working. As women, we can view our lives in seasons. God gives us these seasons to mature and teach us. Each segment of our life is in preparation for what is to come next. Embrace the seasons of your life. Learn, grow and mature with God. Be attentive to His voice. He will use every life experience for your good and His glory (Romans 8:28). Whatever and wherever God has you, it is not by accident. You are there to make an impact, even if it's just for one person.

Look back at the Purpose Discovery Assessment. What is your purpose? Perhaps, your current job or career has nothing to do with your purpose. Do not get discouraged, because even in your present place of employment God can use you. My aim is to equip women and for years there I was at home with my three kids. How was I supposed to impact women? As I began to get more comfortable with my homeschooling, I realized I could help the newer moms who were starting their journey. So, that's how I was able to impact women. As a pastor's wife, there are numerous opportunities to impact the lives of women, and sometimes it is just by being a role model, an example for others to follow.

Your purpose is your calling or vocation. The word vocation comes from the Latin root meaning, "to call." Pray and ask God to show you opportunities and possibilities to use your purpose right where you are. He will be faithful to answer your prayer.

Cultivate

In everything we do, we must have an excellent spirit and do all things in excellence. "Whatever you do, do your work heartily, as for the Lord rather than for men; knowing that from the Lord you will receive the reward of the inheritance. It is the Lord Christ whom you serve" (Colossians 3:23-24).

When you use your gifts to serve God, you need not look for man's applause. And when you do receive the recognition or praise of man, do so with humility.

Previously, we discussed the difference between perfection and excellence. You will remember that excellence is not doing something perfectly, but doing it well. It is a process, and you perfect your gift every time you utilize it.

Keep cultivating or improving your talent. Look for ways to learn and keep growing to develop the gifts God has given you. The possibilities are endless;

colleges offer a variety of courses for the general public to participate in, and many online courses are only a click away.

Release Your Gifts

Your gift is not for you alone. Share it with others. We are the body of Christ, and there are many members. We each have a part to play, and it is imperative that we work together. I may have a gift that you don't have, and on the other hand, you may have a gift that I don't have.

Consider how you can use your gift in your home, place of employment, or in your local church. You can even go further and look for places to volunteer. Perhaps you enjoy reading to children. I know that many public schools welcome volunteers to come and read to their elementary classes. What an opportunity to touch a child's life. You may not be able to share the gospel, but just being there, your very presence can be a shining light. A hug or a smile can mean the world to a little child. Let them see Jesus in you.

"As each one has received a special gift, employ it as serving one another, as good stewards of the manifold grace of God" (1 Peter 4:10).

As we have discovered the seven pillars of a noble woman, our journey together has come to a close. I have enjoyed sharing some insight and practical ideas with you. I pray dear sister and friend that your journey does not end here. It is my hope and desire that you will take these principles and implement them in your daily life. You are a noble woman. Journey on to become a woman of distinction.

My Prayer for You

Dear Father,

I ask you to bless my sister, my friend. I pray that she has received your revelation and knowledge. The words on these pages are not mine, but yours, Oh God. I have been humbled to have been the instrument to pen these words.

I pray each woman who reads this book will realize the potential she has to be a noble lady. You have created her to be unique and valuable. You have placed inside of her the purpose for her life. Help her to discover her purpose and to live out her purpose for your glory and honor.

Oh God, let her know how much you love her and delight in her. Her past does not define her. Her identity is in you, and she has been perfected in you. Just like Esther, she too was created for such a time as this.

May she embrace the qualities of virtue that have been placed within her. May she rise above the norm and walk in confidence. Give her peace and strength to press through the pressures of life. Help her to stand tall and trust you when the world tells her to conform.

God, let her know that all things are possible with you. You have promised in your Word never to leave her nor forsake her.

I ask you, God, to bestow your favor upon your noble daughter.

In Jesus' Name,

Amen

- Where I am right now is not where I will always be.
- My purpose is my calling.
- Excellence is a process.
- Cultivate skills.
- Release my gift.

PROCLAMATION

- I will make an impact in my current position.
- I will embrace my season of life.
- I will do all things in excellence.
- I will cultivate my gifts.
- I will share my talents.

Personal Reflection

1. Evaluate your season of life. How can you embrace this time in your life?

2. What can you do to make an impact? It can be something small. Do you have a special recipe? Can you make something for your co-workers?

3. Read Colossians 3:23-24. How does this scripture change your perspective?

4. How can you cultivate and enhance your skills? Explore the options and do your research.

Final Thoughts

I read this quote on a church sign, and I had to let it sink in, "A wish changes nothing. A decision changes everything" (author unknown). How true, so often we go through life, "wishing." We wish we could be more organized, eat healthier, be a better mother or wife, and be more intentional. But as long as we are only wishing, nothing is going to happen. Everything will remain the same. A wish does not motivate action or intention. It's just a thought that lies dormant.

You have to make the decision to make the changes you want to see in your life. It can be scary. Once you decide to make some changes, you need to create a plan, sit down and write down some goals. In saying that, I realize setting goals can also be intimidating. For me, I find it easier to be a problem solver than a goal setter. So, I look at things I want to do and develop a plan to overcome the obstacles that could stop me from solving my problem.

For an example, if I decide I want to pursue a healthier lifestyle and eat more fruits and vegetables. The way that I can accomplish this is to figure out what the obstacles are. Well, maybe I don't eat enough fruits and vegetables because I don't know how to prepare them to suit my tastes. So, I need to find recipes and creative ways to incorporate these into my everyday meal planning.

Perhaps you are a goal setter who likes focusing

on the steps to reach your goals. It will be necessary for you to create steps to achieve your goals. Both methods work; it just depends on your personality. What matters is that you achieve the results you desire to see.

Go back through the book and choose one pillar to establish in your life. Start with one that is not too challenging and either focus on the obstacles you need to remove or focus on the steps to get you where you want to go.

Let me also make you aware of four things that can hinder your progress. They are **familiarity, facts, feelings, and fear**. Familiarity is staying in your comfort zone, doing what is familiar. You settle for the "norm" and achieve nothing. You are merely existing. You have to rise above what is familiar and do something different to soar.

People will inevitably want to remind you of the facts. They may even say negative things to you, reminding you of your past shortcomings. Yes, the facts are there, but you must rise above the facts and face the truth. The truth is your identity is in God, and regardless of how anyone sees you, you are a noble woman. Remember that illustration of the twenty-dollar bill? The facts cannot deny your value or worth.

Our feelings can get us into a whole heap of trouble. Your emotions were given to you as a way of expressing what is inside of you. They were never there for you to base or make your life decisions. You cannot steer your life on feelings. You must rise above the feelings and live your life by principles. Feelings will come and go; principles will last forever. You will make wise choices and decisions when you base them on standards.

We cannot live our lives driven by fear. Fear will steal opportunities from our lives. It will paralyze us and enable us from moving forward. There are numerous scriptures in the Bible that begin with the words, "Fear not," reminding us that we do not need to be afraid. Instead of falling into the clutches of fear, let us pursue to live our lives by faith. "Fear debilitates; faith liberates." *(Sylvia Banks)*

God told Moses in Deuteronomy 31:6, "Be strong and courageous, do not be afraid or tremble at them, for the Lord your God is the one who goes with you. He will not fail you or forsake you." These words still hold true for each of us. It takes strength and courage to be a noble woman, but our God is with us, and He will never leave us.

Let us boldly lift up the banner of authentic nobility and become women of distinction. Let us not lose the art of feminine grace and the beauty of womanhood. We need to be role models for the younger generation of ladies. Many do not have women in their lives who can guide and mentor them. Take these seven pillars, live them out and share them. Together we can restore women back to their nobility one woman at a time.

Works Cited

Banks, David L. "Personal Purpose Discovery Assessment." 2008.

Banks, David L. Ph.D. "The Making of a Noble Woman." Chattanooga, 15 November 2015.

Berg, Pat. "quietinganoisysoul.com/Perfectionism vs. Biblical Excellence." 1992. *quietinganoisysoul.com.*

Covey, Stephen R. "Everyda Greatness." Nashville: Rutledge Hill Press, 2006.

George, Elizabeth. *Beautiful in God's Eyes*. Eugene: Harvest House Publishers, 1998.

Greenspan, Thomas. *Moving Past Perfect.* n.d.

KJV Dictionary. n.d.

Lybrand, Dr. Fred Ray. "Stop Setting Goals if you would rather solve problems." 17 March 2014.

Maxwell, John C. *The 21 Indispensable Qualities of a Leader*. Nashville: Thomas Nelson, 1999.

michaelhyatt.com. n.d.

Middletownbiblechurch.org/homefam/prov31.htm. n.d.

Monica A. Frank, PhD. *excelatlife.com*. n.d.

Omartian, Stormie. *The Power of a Praying Wife*. Eugene: Harvest House Publishers, 1997.

The New York Times. "well.blogs.nytimes.com." 12 August 2013. *well.blogs.nytimes.com.*

About the Author

Sylvia received her BA in psychology from Bryan College in Dayton, TN. She taught pre-kindergarten for three years and the past sixteen years has been a teacher at Banks Academy of Excellence. She also teaches at the Catoosa Homeschool Co-op.

She is a Certified Family Coach. She also coaches women on how to attain and implement organizational and time management skills to provide a structure into their lives and homes. She also serves as a mentor to home homeschool mothers.

She enjoys writing and has authored devotionals, poems, articles and has developed two course studies for women, *Women of Excellence* and *Time for Order.* She has assisted in editing three published books. Crafting and being creative are also hobbies Sylvia enjoys.

Servanthood is a part of Sylvia's character and nature. Her various roles at the church include serving as a pastor's wife, Director of Children's Ministry, Hospitality Coordinator and Administrative Assistant.

Sylvia and David have been happily married for twenty-six years. They have three children and make their home in Tennessee.

An Invitation to Connect

Sylvia would enjoy hearing from you and invites you to connect with her.

Visit: www.noblewomen.net

Address: P.O. Box 80754
Chattanooga, TN 37414

Email: sylbanks@gmail.com